THE GROWTH FILES

Jane Oma

THE GROWTH FILES

Identify, Unearth, Refine and Unleash
the Powerful You

Jane Oma

Edited and Published in Nigeria by SW Advantage Resources
14, Frajend Close, Osborne Foreshore Estate, Ikoyi, Lagos State.
www.sw-advantage.com, edits@sw-advantage.com,
+2348037741008

This one is for you, Mummy.
The one who tilled and nurtured me.
The one who taught me wholly about growth.
Thank you, Mum, for the gift of the clan (my
siblings), who have become my anchor and
reminders.

Acknowledgements

There are many people without whom this book would not have seen the light of day. Noteworthy among them are:

My sister, Chioma and all my siblings, my nephews and nieces, whose love and covering keep me rooted in my core values.

Those who have served me as mentors, teachers, and positive influences.

Those who have trusted me to serve them as mentor and advisor—challenging me to stay authentic, honest and humble while unearthing, refining, and manifesting the best version of myself every waking moment.

To my publisher—Ini Akpan—and her team, thank you for your patience as we worked through every sentence and every sentiment.

Thank you all.

Introduction

Wherever you are in life, growth can and will happen. Nature makes it so.

Whether you just achieved something significant or just failed at something, each stage presents you with a new opportunity for growth. Every time you accomplish something significant or reach a peak in your journey, life presents you another mountain to climb or difficulty to subdue.

Growth is an unending cycle and a necessary part of life.

Whether as a young high school graduate or the CEO of a global conglomerate, you will always be confronted with new situations and fresh opportunities for growth. You will always need to evolve into a wiser, stronger, better, and perhaps more resolute version of you, even in retirement.

I hope the thought of continuous growth does not scare you. Do not let it scare you because the principles for becoming the most powerful version of yourself at every stage of your life are quite elementary. For example, to grow in your personal life, there are a few things you will absolutely need in your arsenal. They include a strong sense of self and identity, clarity of purpose and a clear direction.

Unfortunately, many of us are not given a manual with which to navigate our different seasons. We often fall into the assumption that we need a different set of tools for each season, but nothing could be further from the truth.

Thus, in our quest for new tools, we barely scratch the surface of whom we could be in each season. We miss out on our best, most authentic and most accomplished selves, flitting from one season to the other with joylessness and discontent.

The primary goal of this book is to provide you with that manual with which you can foster continued growth—as you understand your true self intimately, unearth your buried treasures, unleash your potentials, and refine your expression at every stage of your journey. I desire for you to continue your growth journey and to be the most powerful and the most fulfilled version of yourself every day and in every way.

No matter where you are in your journey, the thoughts and principles I share in this book will help you navigate with ease, as they have helped the ninety-one people with whom I have shared these thoughts in a structured mentoring programme in the last five years. I have observed them transition from one level to another and in many cases, from one expression to another, finding joy and fulfilment every time they unearth a treasure in their own lives.

Finally, this is not a book of regulations or a map to be followed with strict precision. In life, variables abound, so it is important to remind yourself that there is never a one-size-fits all guide for living.

Approach this book, therefore, as a manual, a guide, or a set of letters from a friend. It is a compilation of proven processes and insights gained from years of exposure to diversity of cultures, backgrounds, beliefs, and faiths. As you read, be sure to pay close attention to your variables, take what you need according to where you are and adapt it to your peculiar circumstance.

Cheers to becoming the greatest version of you!

Contents

PART 1

Our goal in life should not be to pursue imagined or externally derived ideals, but rather to develop a more realistic understanding of our strengths and limitations.
–
Jane Oma

1

The Identity Question

'Knowing yourself is the beginning of all wisdom.'

– Aristotle

Dear One,

Who are you?

When was the last time anyone asked you that question? And when was the last time you asked someone the same question? It's an odd one to ask, isn't it? However, it is one of the most crucial questions you will answer on your journey. There will always be someone who asks you this question.

So, who are you? I would love you to reflect on that question and assess how it makes you feel as well as how you respond.

You may stutter in response or you may have a ready answer depending on your level of self-awareness.

To become the best and most powerful version of yourself, the first and most important step is to know who you really are. You have to be certain of your identity at any given time.

Identity is the distinguishing character or personality of an individual. *Psychology Today* describes 'Identity' as 'encompassing the memories, experiences, relationships, and values that create one's sense of self.'

Your identity is internal and personal. It includes your thoughts, beliefs, opinions, moral attitudes, and core values, all of which directly determine and dictate the choices you make in every area of your life, including your relationships, career, etc. These choices, in turn, reflect who we are and what you value.

Identity is the set of qualities, beliefs, personality traits, appearance, and/or expressions that characterize a person or group. In psychology, the term *identity* is most commonly used to describe personal peculiarity, or the distinctive qualities or traits that make an individual unique. Identities are strongly associated with self-concept, self-image (one's mental model of oneself), self-esteem, and individuality.

Your sense of self and identity are influenced by the many relationships you are exposed to and cultivate over the periods of your life. These include but are not limited to your identity as a child, friend, peer, partner, parent, and community member.

Identity also involves external characteristics over which you have little or no control, such as your height, race, or socioeconomic class. However, these are only a little part of the tip of the iceberg of identity—the visible part which people see.

A combination of the things you do also add up to how your identity is expressed and shared with the world around you. These include your talents, your gifts, your strengths, your weaknesses, the things you are passionate about, the things you love, the things you care about, the things you devote time, attention and resources to, and so on.

The work of Psychologist Erik Erikson (1950) defines identity as referring to either

(a) a social category, defined by membership rules and (alleged) characteristic attributes or expected behaviours, or

(b) socially distinguishing features that a person takes a special pride in or views as unchangeable but socially consequential (or (a) and (b) at once).

In the latter sense, 'identity' is a modern formulation of dignity, pride, or honour that implicitly links these to social categories.

A clear definition and understanding of your identity positions you differently in the world with a rare kind of wisdom, confidence, and the uncanny ability to create room for what you want out of life. This clarity then positions and propels you to align your external reality with your internal convictions.

The truth is that when you know who you are, it makes a lot of difference in the way you live your life. Knowing who you are will help you to know what makes you the person you are—the beliefs, exposures and experiences that have contributed to your internal compass and makeup—spiritually, mentally, and otherwise.

Answering the identity question helps you address who you are and gives you an insight into who you can be, your potentials and talents while putting them to work in a way that makes you better.

> Answering the identity question helps you address who you are and gives an insight into who you can be.

Another benefit is that it helps you to know how you evolve and how to do so in a way that positively impacts you and the people in your sphere of influence.

So, how do you define who you are?

Often, people make the mistake of defining themselves based on the things they do. But the truth is that who you are goes beyond what you do. Your actions do not just happen; you do not just do things. Everything you do is generally propelled by something greater.

An accumulation of your actions create the results

which others see, which then determine how they describe or define you.

In other words, your sense of identity informs your beliefs, your beliefs influence your behaviour, and your behaviour creates your results. But if you do not first understand your identity or what fuels your beliefs, you would become a wishy-washy human being, blown around by every doctrine, opinion, and suggestion.

Worse still, you may find yourself constantly wondering why you do the things you do. You may even find yourself apportioning blames but never taking responsibility for your choices and the consequences.

There's also the mistake of allowing your identity to be defined by other people and other external factors. Parents, siblings, spouses, children and other family members, friends, teachers, bosses, colleagues, peers, acquaintances and even strangers may all speak into your life with their various opinions.

Oftentimes, a good number of these people come from a good place and with good intentions, but you must constantly remind yourself that you are the only one who has the responsibility to figure out who you are. Only *you* have the responsibility to define who you are.

I recall a popular fable of the eagle and the chicken. The story tells of a farmer who found an eagle that had fallen from its nest and took the injured bird home to nurse it. He placed the eagle among his chickens and soon the bird recovered. However, because it was confined to the coop with the domestic birds, the king of birds grew up behaving like a chicken.

One day, a naturalist visited the farm and noticed the eagle among the chickens. The farmer explained to him that it had never learned to fly. It had been trained to be a chicken and was therefore no longer an eagle.

The naturalist knew better and said, 'Its true identity is still that of an eagle and it can be taught to fly.' Then he took the bird in his hands, raised it towards the sky and said, 'You belong to the sky. Spread your wings and fly.'

The eagle glanced down at the coop below and jumped down, comfortable to join the chickens in rummaging for worms on the ground.

The naturalist knew the bird was made for something better. He took the eagle to the rooftop and prompted it to fly. But the eagle jumped down to join the chickens, full of fear and unaware of its identity and potential.

Finally, the naturalist brought the eagle to a mountain. He held the bird above his head, saying, 'You are an eagle! Spread your wings and fly.' This time, the eagle stared upwards into the bright sun. It straightened its body, stretched its wings and began to flap them. Then with a mighty screech, it flew into the sky and soared high above the chickens. The eagle had discovered its identity.

Had the eagle not discovered itself, it would have remained in the farm among chickens, behaving like a chicken as tagged by the farmer.

Knowing and being conscious of your identity sets the tone for the outcomes you produce in life. I am certain that you have seen people wanting to copy what others are doing to get the results those others are getting. And, of course, they fail woefully. Please remind yourself that you do not need to replicate anyone else's results. You must not try to twist yourself into becoming someone else. You are enough. You came fully equipped to be enough.

Knowing your identity is vital if you must make headway in life. When you allow yourself to be solely defined by others, you end up with different versions of yourself as described by other people. When you accept the labels and definitions that other people place on you, you make yourself a passenger in your own life, only tagging along for the ride.

It bears repeating that the only person who can and should define you is you.

Identity, a Dynamo

2

'We know what we are, but not what we may be.'

– William Shakespeare

Having understood the basic concept of identity, you may be tempted to think that identity does not change.

Many believe that their identity is fixed within them. You may often hear statements like, 'This is who I am and this is how I am. This is my personality. I was born this way. I woke up this way…'

It is not true. Your identity is constantly evolving. As you evolve, your identity evolves, and as your identity evolves, you also morph in adaptation to your corresponding needs. So, your identity will become one thing or the other at different stages of your life.

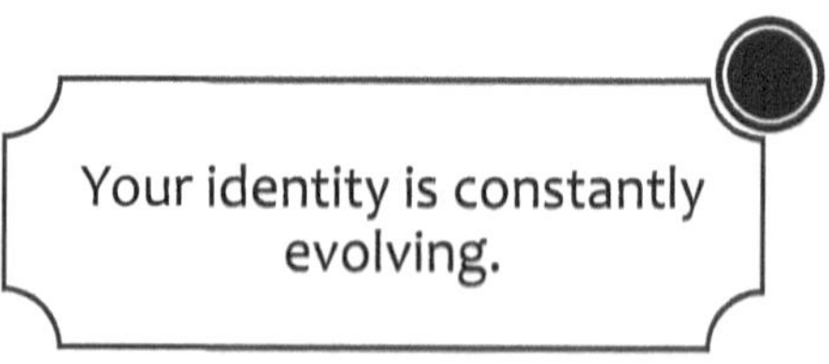

In one of his letters to the Church, Paul wrote: 'When I was a child, I spoke like a child, I thought like a child, and I acted as a child. And now that I am an adult, and becoming an adult, I am acting as an adult.'

This depicts the true nature of identity.

In the book, *The Transformation of Learning: Advances in Cultural-Historical Activity Theory* (Reissue Edition), the author has this to say about how adults learn and how it ties up to our sense of identity:

Identity is not static, but dynamic; it evolves and constantly develops in various social practices. Identity is not an objective feature of a person, but a discursive one constructed continually by social interactions in daily situations in which an individual lives.

Exposure Matters

Before you sow a seed, you will till the ground and fertilise it. After planting the seed, you either pray for rain or make efforts to water the ground. Why do you do these?

It's because you know there are nutrients you must put into the soil for the seed to grow. The richness of the soil will determine the seedling's growth, and as it grows, it will sprout. In addition to the soil quality, how you nurture the plant after the sprouting stage will determine your harvest at the end of the season.

In the same way, your identity at every stage is influenced by the quality of the exposure and experiences you allow yourself to have.

For this reason, you must be intentional about the things you expose yourself to because that will affect the next version of who you become. Nurture your mind by reading, studying, and connecting with people who can help you.

The people you interact with, the books you read, the places you visit, your neighbourhood, where you school, etc. have a big influence on who you become in the next level of your life. Whatever you expose yourself to directly impacts your ever evolving identity.

Step by Step

Life is lived in stages. At every stage, you unveil a new part of who you are, sometimes based on what you learned from a previous stage. Once you're done with that stage, you move on to the next stage with your lived experiences, your exposure and all the lessons you picked along the way.

To be the greatest version of yourself that you can ever be, your identity at every stage has to be wholly developed before you move to the next stage. This is important because the next stage may demand change, evolution, or different applications of the lessons you have acquired.

You must also remember that your needs, environment and abilities will be different at each stage. As you grow in life, so will your identity and how it is expressed.

Dear One, please remember that identity is not static. It constantly develops.

You can liken this to the way a seed grows. On its own, it remains an untarnished seed. When you plant it in soil, it germinates and begins to change its structure, developing roots and pushing them into the ground. When it starts to sprout, it takes on another shape and behaviour, growing stems and shooting upwards towards the sky. At every stage, it behaves exactly as it is supposed to behave, then it moves onto the next stage.

If it fails to behave as a seed, you are not going to have a seedling. If it behaves like a seed and fails to behave as a seedling, you are not going to have a plant. If it fails to behave as a plant, it will not bear fruit. When it is time to bear fruit and it doesn't, you are not going to have a harvest.

Every part of your evolution that you try to deny or stifle will directly determine how you manifest your next level.

In essence, when you are a child, don't try to be an adult. Be a child, fully experience and enjoy your childhood. Learn from it. Then when you become a teenager or an adult, rinse and repeat.

Every part of your evolution that you try to deny or stifle will directly determine how you manifest your next level.

No matter where you find yourself, take ownership and responsibility for that stage of your identity.

While it is important to prepare for the next stage of your life, it is even more important that you are fully and actively present in every stage of your life. Do not waste energy or resources trying to dwell in a stage of life that you have outgrown. In the same way, do not become obsessed with wishful thinking about a stage of life that you have not yet attained.

When you're single, live fully as a single person. When you are married, live fully as a married person who is now sharing their life with someone else. When you have children, also live fully. No matter what stage you are in your life today, decide to live it fully.

It is in doing so that you learn the valuable lessons that will help you define who you want to be in the next stage of your life.

Nothing Left to Chance

With every new height you attain, you have to consciously determine who you want to be. You need to be clear about who you want to be as a start-up business owner with one team member, a business leader with ten team members, a new employee, a member of a small team, one who is making a million dollars, or one who is invoicing one hundred million dollars.

Know that moving to the next stage does not invalidate the events of the previous stage. Relating this to the seedling illustration, when the plant sprouts in its seedling stage, it does not invalidate anything that has happened to it during its seed stage.

Sometimes, you may want to pretend like something that happened at a particular stage of your life did not happen. Embrace the reality. It happened, and that's how taking ownership and responsibility begins.

Consider this. While climbing stairs, you've got to take one step, another, yet another, and the next until you get to where you are going. You cannot get to the top of the stairs without climbing the lower steps in sequential order.

Also, when you have climbed the stairs, they will not disappear. No. Someone else will come after you who will use those stairs to also get to their destination. You may also need to descend the same stairs to get to your next destination.

Embracing the reality of your experiences also helps you to pay attention to the lessons you learn because in understanding your identity, you may realise that negative experiences are not so bad as long as you are not stuck there.

When you look back, it must be to learn something that will help you to move forward. So, if you're looking back at something you've regretted doing, it would be to remind you not to do it again. And if you're looking back at something that has worked for you, it will be to ask yourself if you can replicate it and if it will still work at the next stage.

In the next chapter, we will discuss an often-misunderstood facet of identity.

3

In Pursuit of Purpose

'Dig deep enough in every heart and you'll find it: a longing for meaning, a quest for purpose. As surely as a child breathes, he will someday wonder, what is the purpose of my life?'

– Max Lucado

Dear One,

As the hunger to know yourself better grows, one of the questions that may pop up in your mind would be, 'Why am I here?'

I am certain that you have heard the word 'purpose' too many times and perhaps you have come to a place where you think it's just something motivational speakers use to stir up people's emotions — positively or negatively. In spite of how you feel towards this topic, the purpose question is an important one.

Purpose is your personally-derived, authentic set of life aims that guides your behaviour, pulls you into the future, and gives meaning to life (Rainey, 2014). It is a core part of your identity and is interwoven with your set of values. Consequently, both purpose and values are characterized as being guides for living a life that is personalised, aspirational, and action-oriented.

Here are a few facts to know about purpose:

• The human need for personal meaning and satisfaction is universal. At different points in the life of every human, one feels the need to asks questions pertaining to the reason for one's existence. Even though these questions might seem ambiguous or unrealistic many times, finding answers to them is the first step to getting personal fulfilment.

• Human nature sees fulfilment as the only true measurement for success or greatness. That is why irrespective of the level you attain, if you do not have this sense of fulfilment in you, it may seem like you are not making progress.

- Fulfilling purpose should be the primary goal of every person.

- Everything in life has a purpose.

- Purpose is the original intent in the mind of the Creator that motivated Him to create a particular item.

- Purpose always precedes production.

- All things begin and end with purpose.

No matter where you are on the journey to understanding and fulfilling purpose, and no matter what you believe, the need for each of us to know our purpose cannot be overemphasised.

Based on my own personal experience and my interactions with people from different backgrounds, cultural dimensions and inclinations, clarity of purpose is as essential as oxygen to the man or woman who wants to live a life of impact.

So, before we go any further, I must ask, 'Do you know your purpose?'

As I interact with people from diverse backgrounds, creeds, cultures, statuses and generations, one thing is clear: a sense of self and an understanding of identity (or the lack of it) is a strong core that determines how we work towards discovering and achieving purpose.

Conversations about knowing who we are and why we are here have often been both straightforward and complex at the same time. You may have heard words like self-confidence, self-esteem, self-control, self-love and so on. These are the ones we consider to be positive. Then there are others which we do not accept to be positive such as selfish, self-centred, self-sabotage, and so on. Understanding and being aware of the word 'self' is key to being in control of the words that follow.

The journey to purpose discovery is a process. You need to consciously identify and walk in the awareness of who you are and what you carry inside you. Doing this is the first step on the journey to real, positive, and sustainable impact.

The quest for purpose begins with a sense of restlessness. Going by the experiences I have had as an individual, a mentor, a leader, or as a team member, I know when people begin to feel restless. At such times, they notice they are no more comfortable with their current situations or locations. They develop the sense that they should be doing more than they are doing at that time.

Once this feeling sets in, the next step is the questioning stage. In subsequent chapters, I discuss in detail what to do at this stage and the next.

I liken purpose discovery to the process of digging. If you want to know your purpose, you've got to dig. This digging isn't going to be a random digging on someone else's land, you've got to dig on your land. You dig when you know there is a treasure to be found on that piece of land.

This digging involves reading, studying, asking questions, talking to people, being curious, exploring, then strategically observing and thinking. From there, you move on to the polishing stage.

This is similar to what happens in the process of refining crude oil. When crude oil is dug out, it goes through a refining process and at the end of the day, ten different products are made from it.

Just like the refining process that crude oil passes through, the treasure you dig out must pass through the refining of the mind, thoughts, expressions, the words you use, the places you go, the people you interact with, how you interact, and how you show up in the world.

It is this refining that determines the quality of each product that you put out. By product here, I mean your purpose. It is the refining process that determines what you come up with. Your purpose is the manifestation the world sees.

> Your purpose is the manifestation the world sees.

Purpose is not something hoisted on you by others. It demands your active participation. Purpose requires you to dig, dig, and dig until you see the gold, diamond and all the treasures you have inside of you.

Purpose is not lost. It is already in you and like your identity, it evolves. There is no end to its discovery. That means that after you have discovered and refined one set of treasures, and used them profitably, you will need to go back again and again to dig up some more, refine and use.

And rinse and repeat until your last breath.

Purpose is a thing of the heart and the mind. You are not going to be able to realise it if your head is not aligned with your heart because those are really where the raw materials are—those are where you need to dig.

In digging, you seek illumination of what lies buried deep within you. It would involve self-examination, which starts from a place of listening—listening to the thoughts that come into your head and choosing what to pay attention to.

We will dig further into this in the next chapter.

The Toolbox

4

'*True self-discovery begins where your comfort zone ends.*'

– Adam Braun

Self-discovery is a progressive journey that entails being at peace with yourself, understanding your place on earth and reaching for the best.

When you have fully discovered your purpose and potential, you may feel inner peace. This means that you have accepted yourself for who you truly are, irrespective of external pressures and you can intentionally begin working on being the best version of yourself.

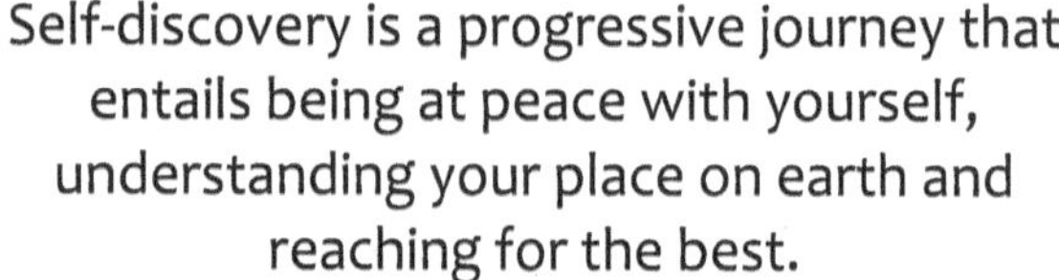

Our goal in life should not be to pursue imagined or externally derived ideals, but to develop a more realistic understanding of our strengths and limitations. By doing so, we can avoid negative psychological states and self-actualise, feel contented, and make better contributions to the world.

Answering the identity and purpose question boils down to having a sense of self awareness, a sense of awareness of others, and an awareness of how all these can impact you as well as how best you can serve your world with that awareness.

Becoming aware of who you are means that you have a deeper understanding of your core identity. It is about being truly honest with yourself without pretending or trying to hide or suppress things. It is about knowing what exactly drives you to do things the way you do them. It sets you on the path to becoming the best and most fruitful version of yourself.

There are tools that can aid your self-discovery, and I have made a list for you below.

1. <u>Curiosity and Introspection</u>

Curiosity plays a big role in defining your identity and purpose. The Cambridge English Dictionary describes curiosity as 'an eager wish to know or learn about something.' Your ability to stay curious is crucial to your identity.

One way to stay curious is by asking questions.

This includes asking questions, not only of others, but also of yourself. To do this, you may have to address yourself in the third person. For example, I sometimes say to myself, *'Jane, why did you do that?'* Asking questions like this takes me to the place of introspection, always.

For me, at this stage, I alternate between asking questions from God, myself, and other people. While asking these questions, I listen, observe, and listen again. It is important to listen again to understand the silent answers. There are answers that are not glaring and can only be gotten when you sit long enough with the questions. Do not be in a haste at this stage so you don't miss out on the important answers you have been waiting for.

You need to understand the importance of introspection in the evolution of identity and purpose. By this, I mean the act of looking inwards and reviewing. During introspection, you ask valid questions such as: *Do I want to be the same person I am today, tomorrow? Have I done what I think is right in my eyes? Am I okay with my choices? Could I have done it better? Is there a better way of doing it?* Nothing must be left to chance. Therefore, introspection is very important.

Part of the work I do involves teaching in Business School, and one of the courses I teach is Multicultural Management. This course has made me understand the concept of the iceberg in how we express ourselves.

When you see an iceberg, what you see is the tip and it's usually just a small portion of it. Most people think the tip is all there is, but underneath the iceberg is a hidden bigger mass. It is this mass, hidden from everyone, that determines the shape of the visible iceberg.

Therefore, when I meet people, I am aware that

there are parts to them that are hidden from me. This awareness stirs my curiosity about what they have underneath, which are the factors that influence their behaviour ranging from family values, upbringing, environment, education, culture, religion, to other things I cannot see.

When you see someone who is elegant, refined, well-spoken and articulate, the reality is that beneath all that may have been good parents, good schools, a lot of books that have been read, several trainings and conferences, a good cultural environment, and a supportive community.

On the other hand, when you see a person who is hot-tempered, that may not be all there is to it. What you see is just the expression when this person explodes. What you do not see are the things happening underneath, which may or may not include previous traumatic experiences, role models who were also hot-tempered and other frustrating life experiences.

When you pay attention to the key ingredients beneath what others see, it makes you self-aware. And it helps you to also know that the same scenario plays out in other people.

Your background, values, and beliefs (under the iceberg) are the things that make up your identity and character, and therefore influence your choices, actions, and results (the visible tip of the iceberg) in everyday life. Understanding how these values and beliefs influence you can help you make better choices.

So, you've got to understand yourself and how you can respond to external cues and triggers.

> Pay close attention to the things you naturally love doing or drift towards, particularly those that are personally expressive. By paying attention to the subconscious pull of these activities, you can allow them guide you toward your true self, stemming from your genetic makeup, upbringing, and experiences (Pagedar, 2021).

The following questions are worth answering as you evaluate yourself:

i. What are your top five personal and professional values?

ii. How are you living your values?

iii. In what areas do you feel a personal sense of responsibility to better the world?

2. <u>External Reports</u>

The quote below captures my thoughts beautifully:

> The more time we spend in the presence of supportive family, friends, lovers, and communities, the sooner we will likely discover our true nature. This is because warm and encouraging atmospheres facilitate feelings of inner security while providing the freedom to have our own feelings and thoughts (Horney, 1950).

You can take out time and learn from family or people whom you think have made a tremendous positive impact in the society. Seek the company of people who inspire you, make you feel positive, and challenge your perception of yourself.

Take care to not let external pressures get the best

of you. Know when to put up the walls against external voices. Set boundaries with people who discourage your individuality, negatively affect your emotions, or put you down.

> When we cannot live in alignment with our true selves, we must spend energy attempting to deny and distort our experiences to make sense of a pervasive lack of happiness and personal fulfilment. This ongoing effort can go so far as to produce psychological states and conditions such as depression (Waterman et al., 2010).

3. Reflection and Meditation

This entails taking notes of your observations and the answers you received in earlier stages.

When I practice these, I give it some time and then go back to look at my notes. I sit back, think about it, and ask myself, 'What am I supposed to be doing? What have I done? How have I come to this point?' I make a comparison of my previous actions and the results they have given me with the strategies I have written. After this comparison is made, I diligently and prayerfully go for the answers that are more productive.

I do these strategically at every point in my life and I have watched myself move from one level of expression of my gift to another.

Meditation has also played a great role in my journey to purpose discovery. In meditation, I shut out all the noise, first from the outside, in order to listen to myself. Next, I shut out the noise from inside and I stay quiet, just breathing, and usually there is a kind of a feeling of calm that comes after each experience. It gives me the feeling of one starting on a clean slate. I have dedicated a whole chapter to this important subject.

Eyes on the Goal

Having done these, dear one, you must remember that the goal is growth. Knowing yourself is only part of the process. Self-awareness provides the map, but you need to get on the road to begin your journey and arrive at your destination.

Identify your abilities and strength, and work on

them. Select values that help you become a better person and find strength and confidence in them.

Define yourself, not merely by what you do (i.e. your profession), but by your values, beliefs and goals. If you merely define yourself by your profession, it limits your abilities. Let's compare these two men. One wakes up every morning, looks in the mirror and tells himself, 'I am a butcher.' The other man wakes up, looks in the mirror and tells himself, 'I am kind, and I hope to make the world a better place. Though I'm a butcher, I can still make the world a better place.'

Any observations?

The person in the first scenario dwells on being just a butcher and making ends meet while the person in the second scenario goes beyond being a butcher.

Do not limit yourself. Set goals, spread your wings and fly as high as you can. The sky is too big and can accommodate all your dreams.

Now, if you are a person of faith, it is important to highlight that identity also entails the understanding of God. So, while you understand self, you should also understand spiritual principles that govern identity.

We will talk more about this in the next chapter.

5

The Faith Connect

Dear One,

Whatever your religious persuasion or lack thereof, you may find this chapter useful because our identities are influenced by factors beyond us.

As a Christian, I believe that who I am is directly connected to who God has said I am. So, I align the understanding of my identity to my understanding of God.

I relate to God as a Father, and to positively define this relationship, I consider my relationship with my earthly dad. This may not apply to those who did not have a great relationship with their dads or those whose dads may have been absent.

In my case, my dad loved us and showed his love in his own way. Even though I lost him many years ago, I still have fond memories of his love, commitment and absolute devotion to us. This relationship has also helped my relationship with God—a unique relationship in every sense that assures me of absolute love and goodness no matter what.

Just like the relationship I had with my dad, in my relationship with God, every day is a new opportunity for me to experience a deeper connection and expression of the love we share. And knowing this manifests in the ways my identity unfolds.

God's word is the anchor upon which I define the core of who I am—from my beliefs to my core values. Like a tree that's firmly rooted in the soil, I take my essence and nourishment from God's word. Like the plant, I dig into the Word regularly and collect what I need for each day or circumstance. And when I get it, I run with it.

In my relationship with the Word, my identity has been and is still being transformed. I visualise that in interacting with the Word, I am like a planted seed which germinates, sprouts, grows branches and leaves, bud flowers, and eventually bears fruits. Depending on the plant, the growth process is often continuous, constantly evolving and ultimately transformative. Each stage of growth unravels new expressions of who I am and who I can be.

I draw insights from God's word which, when applied to every aspect of life, provides me with wisdom, grace, patience, strength and encouragement. I receive grace when I am running low, and I receive wisdom which helps me not to do stupid things. It also helps me remain patient as I am reminded that regardless of what I face in life, it will work out for good for me.

In this journey of discovering identity for growth, the word of God has become a sure tool for getting instructions for life and living.

Oftentimes, there is a lot of noise around. Sometimes, it seems everyone is talking, everyone has a message to share. It gets so noisy that if you do not know who you are, the noises will bring confusion instead of clarity. That is why it's important to understand who you are as well as the voices speaking to you.

To be able to sieve through the noise, you have to master the ability to stand still in a marketplace and hear exactly what you need to do and how you need to do it.

I believe this access is available to everyone, no matter how you choose to profess your faith. The word of God can help you to be still, calm, and to shut out the noises in a way that allows you to listen to the voice that is carrying the instruction you require for the moment. I am also aware that God speaks to us through some people as well.

I have talked about quieting down to listen for the voice of instruction. However, there may be times when having received instruction or after clarifying the voice giving you the blueprint, you may not like the instruction. When this happens, is it possible to go to God to request for it to be changed? Do you have the innate power to work out the change you desire? I do not have a 'yes' or 'no' response but would like to explain so you can make an informed decision.

In the Bible, God says through Isaiah, 'Come let us *reason together...*' When you want to *reason* with someone, you think together, dialogue with the person, and try to convince them of your opinion. Reasoning together implies partnership. It is not a scenario where one party issues instructions while the other party just listens. In requesting that we reason together, it implies that God is willing to be convinced. Even in Scriptures, there are many instances where God changed his mind about different things in response to man's requests.

With this understanding, when there is something I do not want, I go to God and tell him. I explain the reasons I do not want it without throwing any tantrums. That way, I reason with him in prayer.

When I moved to Spain—a non-English speaking country—I didn't know how to speak Spanish. I was a newlywed with lots of ideas in my head about the kind of marriage, home and family I was going to build and the kind of things I wanted to do. In addition, I wanted to go back to school, Few months after I applied for my residency visa, I got it. It was such a miracle and it felt like God approved of all my plans.

In spite of this, several months after I arrived Spain, I felt incapacitated. I had no one to talk to because of the language barrier. The television programmes were in Spanish, my neighbours were Spaniards, I did not know anybody, and I had no friends. For almost three months, I had no contact with any living human being that I could talk to except my husband.

Migrating to a new country is a complicated and demanding process, involving a multitude of practical, economic and emotional challenges resulting from leaving one's homeland, moving to a host country and establishing a new life there.

Accumulated stress associated with the different phases of migration has been found to have a negative impact on immigrants' physical and mental health, and their capacity to adapt to the new environment. The first thing that hits you strongly as you leave your country to another in search of greener pastures is the sting of loneliness. This feeling can make one depressed.

Now you are in a new place that is different from what you are already used to and with a different cultural and religious background from yours. Adjusting to this new life is quite difficult until you meet someone who really understands you.

Adapting to a new system and learning a new language can be an uphill task. It takes a lot of determination and dedication to pass this hurdle.

You would have to create a balance between your background and the new life. You would need to learn currency conversion and how the labour force works. You also need to have a basic knowledge of the constitution to avoid violation of laws and subsequent penalties associated with that.

Because I knew the kind of life I wanted to live, I knew I had to learn the language. I enrolled at a Spanish school and began learning. I started socialising with Nigerians and the African community in Spain. During these interactions, I was made to know that the country was tough. I recall someone asked me to remove the letter 's' from the word 'Spain' and that what I would have left (pain) best describes the country.

I was, and still am, well-spoken and articulate, but many people I met then weren't so articulate. The norm then was to just get a job at a warehouse where all you do is package goods or get a job as a cleaner. Most males I knew were working as security men, cleaners, or labourers on construction sites. For someone like me who was planning to return to school, it seemed impossible to build a career in my preferred field of study.

So, I returned to God and told him, 'This is not the kind of life I want to live. If this is what this place holds for me, I will return to Nigeria.' Right there, I felt Him impressing on my spirit that I could be whatever I wanted to be. Right then, I knew it was in my hands.

I got the message clearly and knew right there and then that I didn't have to be a cleaner if I didn't want to. Now, there's nothing wrong with being a cleaner; it is a legal and respectable job but that wasn't what I wanted.

Today, I'm a management consultant in a country where there are only a few people like me in the company where I work. In fact, I was the first black woman in one of the companies I consulted with. In several other companies where I work, I am and have been either the first black person or the first black woman. People see me and ask, 'How did you do it?' I tell them, 'I reasoned with God. I asked for something different.'

I don't know if it was in the books that every immigrant who came here was to be a cleaner or do menial jobs, but I went to God and said 'No.' I asked for what I wanted, and I got it by His grace. People have changed their trajectory by reasoning with God and putting in the work.

> People have changed their trajectory by reasoning with God and putting in the work.

Whenever I read the portion of Scriptures that says, 'I have given you the power to get wealth,' I realise it is something that applies to everyone, but not everyone uses that power.

If you are in a position where you are thinking, '*This is who God has made me. This is my life. This is what I am going to do,*' you may want to ask God, 'Is this really it?'

It is possible that when you go to ask God, He would say, 'No, that's not it. That's what you're seeing because you're looking at it from your perspective.'

In such a situation, God may change your perspective so you can see differently. Whether it involves changing the plan or changing your position to see the plan differently, you have the innate power to work out the change that you desire.

But you have to ask, you have to listen, you have to dialogue, you have to reason, and you have to put in the work. And that's the only time that you can create change—whether in your own life or in the life of others around you.

64

Fine-Tune Your Compass

1. How do you define yourself?

____

____

____

____

____

____

____

2. How can you ensure your identity is not solely defined by others?

____

____

____

____

____

3. What does purpose mean to you?

____

____

____

____

____

4. Recount a time when you felt restless about your journey and what role did that restlessness play in helping you find purpose?

____

____

____

____

____

____

____

____

5. Knowing that identity is not static, what is your current identity?

____

____

____

____

____

6. Apart from the tools discussed in chapter three, what other tools can you employ for self-discovery?

____

____

____

____

7. What necessary change do you want to see in your life?

____

____

____

____

PART 2

'Clarity is the most important thing. If you are not clear, nothing is going to happen. You have to be clear: Then you have to be confident about your vision. And after that, you just have to put a lot of work in.'

—

Diane Von Furstenberg

6

Turn on the Switch

*'A man with clarity reaches his goal sooner
than the man with confidence.'*

– Sunday Adelaja

Dear One,

I have spoken a lot on the matter of listening to yourself. This is because it is an important step to gaining clarity.

In the quest to live your best life, clarity cannot be overemphasised. As a human being, the only time you will not require clarity is when you have exited this earth. This means that as long as you are alive and growing, you must seek clarity.

The dictionary meaning of clarity is 'clearness or lucidity as to perception or understanding; freedom from indistinctness or ambiguity.'

Clarity is light. When it gets dark, you switch on the light so you can see, and when it's daytime, you have the daylight to make things bright. No wonder in the Biblical record of the beginning of time, God's first utterance was, 'Let there be light.'

Clarity is seeing; not just seeing but seeing well. Some people see but have blurry vision and so, they stagger in their walk, miss their steps, and encounter mishap.

Beyond light, clarity is the active use of light to see, understand, and activate what is inside of you. Clarity eradicates the confusing lines of doubt, ambiguity, or uncertainty.

There are times in your life when you certainly knew there were things you should change regarding your health, finances, business, job, location, mindset, or your approach to life and relationships. But you probably stopped at knowing you had to change things. You didn't know exactly where and how that change was supposed to happen. You had no idea what to do about any of them. Perhaps you ended up either ignoring the things you knew you should change or pretending everything was okay.

For some people, they may not even know that they should change anything. They just go through life unhappy about the results and outcome they are creating, with no clue about what might be wrong or that something might even be wrong. These people do not see another way to live. There is no clarity.

Clarity is seeing what is inside of you, what is ahead of you and what is around you. It has to do with knowing what you can do with all that you see and how you are supposed to effect it.

Clarity is seeing what is inside of you, what is ahead of you and what is around you.

Clarity is knowing that you are not stumbling around without a sense of direction. It is being able to see what to cling to and what to let go of. Clarity is being able to find ways as well as the strength to get yourself back on track when (not *if*) you miss your way or take a wrong turn.

Sometimes, you will see with the light of the day. Sometimes, you will need to switch on a light bulb or a torch. At other times, it would be a lantern held up by someone else. Sometimes, it could be the stars in the sky, the moon or even a flash of lightning. This is to illustrate that clarity will always be there even though you might receive it in different ways at different times.

This is the point. If we do not see clearly, we are bound to grope through life, zigzagging from one thing to another without a sense of direction.

It is like driving around an unfamiliar territory without a map. This will result in missteps, mistakes, misplaced efforts, wasted resources, wasted time, and disappointments.

While there are many lessons, skills, knowledge, and insights to be gleaned from every mistake or change in direction, not having clarity or a clearly defined goal and intention slows your pace and diminishes your resources and subsequently, your outcome.

According to Behavioural Scientist, Steve Maraboli, 'It is a lack of clarity that creates chaos and frustration. Those emotions are poison to any living goal.'

You need clarity to clear darkness and/or ambiguity. According to Kent Sanders, there are many benefits of clarity. They include:

1. Energy

Clarity gives you energy because you know who you are, why you are here, whom you are serving, and what you should be doing. That knowledge and confidence gives you tremendous momentum to overcome all kinds of challenges. It puts a spring to your steps as you step out to do what you need to do. Clarity matters a lot more than you realise.

2. Direction

Imagine you're standing in a room with ten open doors, and you're wearing a blindfold. How can you choose the right door when you can't even see clearly? You will stand there paralysed because you wouldn't want to make the wrong choice. But the more you know yourself and what you're here to do, the more you can recognise which doors are closed and which ones are open.

When you have clarity in your life, it's like removing

the blindfolds of confusion and apathy. It helps you to see what is possible, and what you can do to make it a reality. It helps you to see your own ability to take every required action. Clarity shows you your potential, your gifts and your capabilities.

3. A Plan

The whole topic of time management and productivity is very frustrating for most people. The reason is not because they're not motivated; rather, it is because their lack of clarity prevents them from being productive. You can't be productive if you don't know what you should be producing in the first place. With clarity, you are able to gain momentum and be effective. When you apply time, resources and effort coherently to a clear goal and immutable intention, your results will be beyond exceptional.

4. Courage

This might be the most important benefit. When you have clarity, you have the courage to say 'no' to commitments that don't align with your vision and priorities. It doesn't mean you suddenly become a selfish ogre who is unwilling to give their time to anyone. But it does mean that you now put more value on fulfilling your creative calling than making everyone else happy.

With clarity, you have a roadmap that highlights exactly where you want to go and how to get there. Clarity shows you where you are at any given time, what you can get from each place and how to get it. So, if you truly want to go as far as you should, get clarity.

7

Filters and Patterns

'Clarity is the moment we see without opening our eyes.'

– Stephanie Banks

Dear One,

By now, you must have realised that clarity is not an option. It is an absolute necessity. There is something I refer to as 'the lens through which we view the world.' It can also be likened to a filter. These lenses or filters mostly determine the views we hold about life and how we respond to issues.

Paulo Coelho tells a story of two firemen who went to put out a small fire. After the fire got under control, they stopped to rest. One of them had his face all smeared with soot, while the other man's face was completely clear of soot.

Which of the two do you think washed his face?

You might think that it would be the one with the dirty face, but you are wrong.

Because how would they know what their faces looked like? How would they know if they needed to wash their faces or not, except by looking at each other?

The fireman with the clear face would look at the other one and assume his face was just as smeared and would go wash his face. The fireman with a smeared face, on the other hand, would look at the other and assume his own face was clear of soot.

When you look at other people, what you see does not always reflect your own reality. Looking outside can be deceptive, misleading and damaging if you base your life's choices solely on what you see on other people. Look within instead.

And when you do look outside, as you sometimes

will, ensure you are looking at and talking to people who can truly see or reflect, not only your reality but also your possibilities.

People will always see things from their own filters and lenses and just like we must constantly clean our physical lenses and filters, we need to constantly clean the lenses and filters through which we view things. Sometimes, we will need to change either the lenses themselves or the frames that hold them, all for the sake of clarity.

Clarity of identity, purpose and direction is one of the greatest gifts you can give to yourself and your world. It is the one thing that will position you to truly live a life of positive impact.

Clarity comes in different ways and at different times. In my experience, I have received clarity on different issues while in the shower or while in the restroom. There have been times when clarity has come to me while talking to someone, while listening to another or even while reading.

It is extremely important to know that clarity requires your awareness and active participation. If you do not ask for it, you will not receive it, even when it is staring at you in the face. If you do not know it is there, you cannot make use of it.

> Clarity requires your awareness and active participation. If you do not ask for it, you will not receive it, even when it is staring at you in the face.

Until you realise that it is dark around you, you may never see the need for light. Until you accept you do not know something about a particular issue, you may never seek knowledge. Until you admit to feelings of ill health, you may never go to the hospital.

In the same vein, until you admit to yourself that you need clarity, you will never open yourself to it. Once you get to this point of acceptance, identifying how you get clarity becomes easier.

Over time, I have experienced many lightbulb moments—instances where I had clarity on issues of life. I will share a few of them.

When I first moved to Spain, I had no clear direction on what I needed to do professionally. Less than a year into my living there, I knew I was not going to be happy just staying at home doing nothing and depending on somebody else; I knew I had to do something. I also knew I had to learn the language. But it was tough.

Not many people could speak English in Spain then. A number of times when I would go out and want to ask for directions, I would approach someone and say, 'Excuse me', all I would hear was, 'Oh, no. No English.'

One day, I met this total stranger and I tried to communicate with him. I got to know he understood a little English, so I told him I could teach him some English while he would teach me Spanish in return. He laughed, I did the same, and we went our separate ways, but that experience stayed with me.

A few weeks later, it became a thing. When I asked people for directions in English and they told me they do not speak English, I would offer to teach them the language. Nobody took me up on the offer but that was a light bulb moment for me. I realised they didn't speak English in this country and since I could teach the language, I could help them learn just the same way others were helping me to learn Spanish.

Most of the time, clarity will come to you when you're busy. It comes when you are out and awake.

If you are sleeping, you are not going to see the light. If your eyes are closed, you are not going to see the light. Until your eyes are open, you are not going to get clarity. Even for people who receive instructions in their dreams, they have to get up, think about it and remember their dreams. If they do not remember those dreams, they will not be of any use to them.

I have experienced many of my lightbulb moments when I have been on the move, sometimes, when I am in front of people.

Eventually, I met someone who was an English teacher in the Official School of Languages, and we agreed to work with each other. I was asked if I was a professional teacher and I replied in the negative. She told me that they pay the most attention to grammar and I explained that I could also help them practice conversations. Just like that, I ended up working with this lady. She told her students about me and several of them contacted me.

Another lightbulb moment happened afterwards. I had an idea that, instead of walking up to strangers and asking them if they would like to learn English, I could do it differently. I wrote the details on a piece of paper, went to a business centre to make photocopies of that paper, then hit the streets and began placing them on their windscreens.

It took a while, but I did get a few people call me to ask for conversation classes to help their children with English homework. Then I had more students referred to me by my friend and before I knew it, I had moved from private teaching to academic teaching, to teaching in the Official School of Languages, to teaching in universities—all inspired from the experience when I spoke with a stranger who could not really speak English.

When I went into advisory and consulting, it was also a similar path. While I was into private teaching, someone said to me, 'Jane, what you are doing right now is beyond teaching, you are actually coaching. This is proper executive coaching.'

At the time, I had never heard about executive coaching, not even the word 'coach' as used in that context. After that conversation, I read up about coaching, enrolled for some programmes and jumped in.

This applies to all areas of our lives.

Clarity is not just about seeing the possibility that something could be done, it is also about taking the first step to doing it and being willing to take responsibility for whatever outcome you produce.

When you have the lightbulb moment, the fact that you see the first step at that moment does not mean that you see the result of that step. Similarly, the fact that you see the end does not mean you are going to see every step you have to take to get there. There is a beginning, an end and everything between. You may not see the in-between until you take the first step and embark on your journey. You gain lightbulb moments while in transit.

Have you received any lightbulb moments yet? In the next chapter, I will share specific things I do to switch on my lightbulbs.

8

The Quest

'Take a step back. Clear your mind. Refresh your perspective.'

– Unknown

Dear One,

Have you identified the areas of your life in which you require clarity? There are essentially four major areas of life where you will always need clarity:

Your Who — Identity
This is the point of clarity about who you are. Since growing and evolving will continue to happen, you

will need light to be aware of who you are becoming and how that is going to play out in your big picture.

Your What — Goals

Once you know who you are, you will also need to know your 'what.'

What is it that you really need/want?

What do you need to do to get what you need/want?

What can you do to make a positive impact?

What will be your legacy?

These are some of the questions that will bubble up as you try to figure out your what. To be able to answer them correctly, you need clarity.

Your Why — Purpose

The 'why' question is one that will always keep popping up if you stay curious.

'Why am I here?'

'Why do I have to...?'

'Why do I want...?'

'Why should I...?'

The why questions are endless, and the answers almost always go quite deep, which is the reason I liken it to digging. Every time you find an honest answer to any why question, you will discover a new layer to the core of who you are. To be able to find the answers to any of those questions, you need clarity.

> Every time you find an honest answer to any 'why' question, you will discover a new layer to the core of who you are

Your How - Actions

Once you figure out your 'who,' 'what' and 'why,' the next big question will be 'how?' What are the specific actions you need to take?

You must have realised by now that clarity is not a one-off event. It is something everyone needs to attain regularly. And this means that the actions steps must be continuous.

So, how do you consistently attain clarity? Here are a few strategic routines to help you consistently have clarity in all areas of your life.

1. Faith

In my quest for clarity, I depend on God's word.

You already know how important faith is to me. You also already know the place of God's word in my life. When it comes to finding clarity in any area of my life, I rely heavily on God's word, having built unshakable faith in that word.

The Bible talks about faith coming by hearing God's word.

Dwelling on God's word and passing everything I believe and say through the veracity of that word keeps me grounded. It opens my eyes to see myself, my life, and the choices in front of me.

2. Introspection

I also engage in the use of introspection. This has to do with looking inside and listening to myself. I have found that many of the answers that we all desperately seek are already inside us.

Whether it is finding the courage to set out on a new path or finding the strength to change existing behaviours and outcomes, the key is inside you. This might sound cliché, but you know that it is absolutely true.

I always say that I tend to psychoanalyse myself a lot. I find time to reflect on everything I do;

sometimes, before I do them, and at other times, immediately after I do them. I reflect on how my actions, responses and behaviours trigger people and circumstances around me. I reflect on the outcomes. Armed with my observations, I define or redefine my patterns of behaviour at that time.

It works for me because I have come to a point in my life where I know when I can trust my voice and when I cannot.

3. Journaling

Another important tool that helps me gain clarity is writing and journaling. Writing helps me visualise and articulate the thoughts in my head and heart. It helps me give expressions to the stirrings of my heart. Many of the things I write are done privately and for my own review and consumption. Occasionally, I am led to share some of my words with the world.

When I write, whether privately or publicly, I just allow my thoughts to unravel. I allow the streams of my consciousness to flow. Then I read what I write again and again. I reflect on them and learn from them. I write the questions that I have, answers that I find, experiences, responses, reflections, and the lessons I learn. Every time, my written words teach and bless me. Sometimes, the words do not appear coherent, but I still write.

Let me give an example. In 2010, I stumbled on something I had written in 2004 when there was no social media. After reading it, I edited a few points and till today, those words guide how I use social media.

4. Openness and Readiness

Another way to get clarity is by being open. Always make room for more.

I understood early in my life that no matter what I am or what I have today, there will always be the possibility of being or having more. I live in constant awareness of growth. For this reason, I make space, I take on an open posture, and I embrace flexibility in heart and in mind.

I am always ready. Openness and readiness are two gifts that keep your heart and eyes open. Clarity can only happen when your heart and eyes are truly open and fully ready.

5. Listening

Surround yourself with people you can share your

heart and thoughts with. It is important to always identify people around you who manifest values that you hold dear. Connect to them and share with them as you grow. Share your thoughts. Share your convictions. Share your questions and your doubts. Share your strengths, your wins, and your fears.

Learn to listen. Listen to God, to yourself, and to others. One of the things my mum taught me was to learn how to listen to myself. She would prompt me to speak to myself and listen over and over again to myself before speaking out. As I grow, I have also learnt to listen to God and to select groups of people who help me on my own journey.

When you identify the group of people mentioned above, whose voices speak goodness and life into your spirit, please learn to listen to them. Sometimes, these people will see a bit further than you currently do and it will be a blessing to have them shine their own light on your path. When you find these people, do well to listen.

Listening does not mean you do everything they say at every time. It simply means that you are given meat to chew on. And as you chew, your eyes and mind will be opened to identify your own path. I reckon that in your own life right now, you also have people into whose life you speak, people who look up to your light when they struggle. The same applies—they will not do or take everything you say to them but listening to you will help them grow stronger teeth.

6. Stillness and Meditation

Many times, when I have lacked light and clarity, instead of groping aimlessly, I decide to simply sit still. It takes wisdom and discernment to know if you can risk groping in the dark until the light comes back on or if you should pause until it does.

I have said in the earlier chapter that clarity often comes when one is up and about, creating or seeking solutions. I have also pointed out habits that cause lightbulbs to come on spontaneously. However, there are times when clarity will come to you in a state of stillness, quietness, and peace; when there is no noise and no one telling you what to do and how to do it. In my personal experience, that's when I hear more from God.

The Bible records that in the midst of a raging storm, Jesus said to the waves, 'Peace, be still.' In the midst of fear, anxiety and turmoil, we need that time of stillness and complete quiet. We need to be still because chaos tends to trigger emotions that blind us to reality.

I often attain these undisturbed states via meditation. Meditation clears my mind and heart of clutter and allows me to sync with myself and with God on a much deeper level. I will share more about meditation in the next chapter.

However you choose to attain clarity, remember this: never measure your realities based on what you are seeing in the lives of those around you. Whether you are starting a new business, a new career, changing direction, trying to scale your business, move up the career ladder, or starting afresh in any aspect of your life, remember to hold on to the clarity you receive per time and to evolve with it.

9

Meditation

'... It is exactly like muddy water left to stand in a glass. Little by little the sediment sinks to the bottom and the water becomes pure.'

– Taisen Deshimaru

Dear One,

I must let you know that meditation is a big part of the strategic routines that help me gain clarity consistently.

In Psychology, meditation is defined as a form of mental practices that are designed to familiarise the practitioner with specific types of mental processes and skills. The dictionary meaning of the word 'meditate' is simply to think deeply about something. While the verb suggests reflection, the act of meditation suggests stillness, mental calmness, and introspection (looking within).

Through meditation, you learn how to truly relax your mind and body. It teaches you how to develop the ability to focus on one thing at a time. The way I see it, meditation addresses the human need to stop, shut out all the internal and external noise, reach for the depth of who you are and draw strength from there to continue working on the results, outcomes and transformations you want.

Meditation trains you to be aware of who you are and provides you with a healthy sense of perspective. It helps you learn to observe your innermost thoughts, feelings and consciousness without judgement, and as you do, it helps you understand those thoughts, feelings and consciousness better.

In meditation, you develop the skills to be fully aware of who you are, where you are at any given time, who you can be, where you can go and how to get there. Being fully aware is almost like a superpower. And what a superpower to have!

Perhaps you are familiar with 'The Serenity Prayer.' It is attributed to an American theologian, Reinhold Niebuhr (1892–1971) and it simply says (in part):

> *God, grant me the serenity to accept the things I cannot change, courage to change the things I can, and the wisdom to know the difference...*

It is in meditation and introspection that you find the wisdom to know the difference between where you need serenity and where you need courage. It is in the place of meditation that you are transported to a higher realm of consciousness you would not have known existed.

Many people think that meditation is prayer, and it is indeed a form of prayer. However, you already know that for many people, prayer is a time when they only tell or ask God what they want Him to do for them or for the ones they care about.

Meditation is not about you telling God or anyone what to do. It is not about making your requests and supplications known to God, which is actually only just one kind of prayer.

Some others think that meditation is staring into

space, thinking about their lives or about their problems. For some, meditation is just thinking about God. Again, meditation is none of the above.

In fact, meditation is not a religious practice. It is something anybody can practice, regardless of their faith, whether they believe in God or have a relationship with Him or not.

Some people think it is about filling your mind with something. Contrary to that, meditation is not supposed to fill your mind with anything. What meditation does is to completely clear your mind.

When done well, meditating becomes a form of prayer that helps you connect with your core and from that core, you are better able to contemplate and create a strong union with God. I speak as a person of faith here; if you do not care much about connecting with God, meditation will help you connect with the best and highest version of yourself.

And yes, it is mostly in the place of deep, quiet meditation that many will tell you they hear God. This is because when your mind and spirit quieten down, you are better able to hear and feel God. It is also when your mind quietens that you truly know, see and hear yourself.

To practise meditation, ensure to be in a quiet place. Find a place where it's just you and your thoughts. Once you start, you build the muscles for it and it becomes a habit.

If you are unable to get a quiet place, you can learn to tune out for two or five minutes in a place as noisy as a marketplace. Even if there is a sound, it has to be a background noise that is slow and like a slur. It could also be music playing in the background at a low volume. It could even be in the bathroom with the sound of water splashing. Just try to create an environment that helps your thoughts.

For me, I go for really soft noise that doesn't scream or distract but flows with my thoughts. This, I consider important for my meditation.

Once you are able to completely clear your mind of the noise outside, and the noise inside, that's meditation. When you get to a point where you can shut the noise inside down, that's a different level of meditation and the moment that noise inside goes off, there is a different level of clarity that you attract.

Another thing that helps my meditation is knowledge. When I find myself learning something new, it makes it easier for me to connect with my own thoughts because when I begin meditating, I find myself thinking about what I had learnt from one encounter or the other. I find it easier to reflect on who I was in the face of that knowledge or encounter, how I behaved, how I should behave, or how I could have done better.

You see, meditation not only inspires clarity and growth in you, it contributes to a more balanced and wholesome life. There are many studies and scientific evidence that show the psychological and physiological effects of meditation. These have shown up in different areas of my own life including:

- My overall wellbeing: improved physical and mental health, improved memory recall, acuity, focus, mindfulness, compassion, empathy, an enhanced ability to give, share, learn, trust and forgive, and to practise a more fulfilling lifestyle.

- My personal growth: emotional well-being, self-awareness, self-discipline, creativity, resilience, a more agile decision-making process, greater rapidity in learning and development skills, managing distractions, increased cognitive retention, ability to manage, relieve or work under stress, increased productivity and performance, among others.

– Spirituality: more ease in connecting with God, listening and hearing God, a stronger sense of inner peace, unwavering faith, ability to recognise the joy inside me, a deeper awareness of my identity, gifts and a clearer understanding of how to apply them at different times.

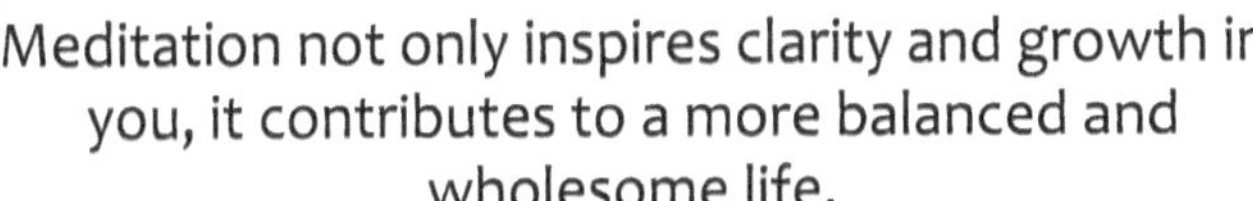

Meditation not only inspires clarity and growth in you, it contributes to a more balanced and wholesome life.

Even though I highly recommend meditation, it is not easy or automatic at the beginning. Someone once shared some of the difficulties she encountered in getting her mind to quieten down. She talked about how frustrated she felt that she couldn't seem to stop her mind from moving to one thought or another, talking, or remembering things that had been said to her in the past. However, she refused to give up and kept trying. After two weeks of daily attempts, she had her first three minutes where she felt her mind quieten completely.

She shared about how transforming that experience was for her. How much she enjoyed the calm and how much clarity she found in it. She has gone on to have fifteen-minute meditations every day, and it forms a crucial part of her day.

The benefits of meditation are wide and varied and like every good thing, you've got to keep at it until it becomes a part of you. You need to make time out of your busy twenty-four hours in a day to connect with yourself.

I do that often because it positions me to start the day from a place of peace and wellness, and believe me, nothing beats that!

Fine-Tune Your Compass

1. What does clarity mean to you?

____

____

____

____

____

____

____

2. What do you stand to benefit from having clarity?

____

____

____

____

____

3. Can you identify the lenses through which you view your world?

____

____

____

____

____

4. How can you recognise a light-bulb moment?

____

____

____

____

5. What areas of your life require clarity?

____

____

____

____

6. What can you do to receive clarity henceforth?

____

____

____

____

____

____

PART 3

'For growth to happen, change will happen; for change to happen, growth will happen.'
—

Jane Oma

10

The Power of Pause

'Nature has the power to heal. By slowing down and letting yourself notice the smell, sound and feel of nature, you become present, aware and often experience less stress. You become unbusy.'

– Lettie Stratton

Dear One,

Discovering your identity and purpose are processes embedded in growth. Growth is regarded as the process of developing physically, mentally, or spiritually. Like discovering identity and gaining clarity, it is not a one-off event. It is continuous.

While it is a constant process, it is not also an easy one. In the midst of all the constant discovery of self and purpose, it is important to PURRR.

No, this is not a typo. While it kind of sounds like something you'd hear from a kitten, this particular word does not refer to the sound of a happy kitten or of one demanding attention.

It is, however, something that if not done right will definitely put you in a place where your mind, body and soul will demand attention from you. And when done right, it will definitely have you purring like a happy kitten as you continue on your growth journey.

Take a look at the word again: P.U.R.R.R. with an extra 'R'. PURRR is an acronym for:

- Pause
- Unknot
- Rest
- Reset
- Rejuvenate

As you navigate life, learn to pause, unknot, rest, reset and rejuvenate from time to time. Knowing the best time to pause boils down to self-awareness. When you know yourself well enough, you know how much you can push yourself. Yes, it's important for us to push ourselves constantly, but it's also important to know when to stop, sit, breathe, and not do things that put you under pressure.

> As you navigate life, learn to pause, unknot, rest, reset and rejuvenate from time to time.

We live in a world where you are likely to often hear, 'Don't quit, don't give up, keep going.' The truth is, for growth to happen, there has to be a time when it will seem as if nothing is happening. Recall the example of the seed. After the seed has been planted, it first seems like nothing is happening, but after some days, depending on the kind of seed it is, you notice it sprouting, then the stem begins to grow. In all these, do not forget there was a time when it seemed like nothing was happening.

Towards the end of the dry season or during autumn, the trees become bare as the leaves completely fall off. All signs of green disappear and everywhere becomes dry. Then the rains return in spring. In the first few weeks of rain, the trees are still bare. Many people do not see when the leaves start coming up again or when the flowers start to bud. What we do see is the lush greenery when the leaves all grow and bloom once the flowers are out. It's all so colourful, seeing the land again. The tree has leaves again and we appreciate the sight. This growth (change) did not happen overnight.

Nature itself teaches us to pause. When the leaves fall, that's a moment of pause. When the rainfall starts but the leaves are still not showing, and the trees are still bare, that's still a moment of pause.

Pause can be activated at any stage of one's life. Life gets busy and before you know it, things come together like a big ball of wire. And suddenly, there is a need to pay school fees, hospital bills, vacation, etc. It can sometimes be overwhelming.

During this period of PURRR, you can decide to go on vacation, take a solo trip, change your environment, and breathe in fresh air to prepare you for the next task ahead. You can also use this period to run an overall test to examine your health. This period can be regarded as the resuscitating period.

For a number of people, the order can change. Some people might pause and rest before they start. Some people cry when they pause and by doing so, they release pent up emotion. The order is not as important as understanding that you do need to PURRR from time to time.

You need to stop, catch your breath, get some rest, examine your thoughts, reorganize them, re-examine them, then re-strategize. That's really what pause is all about.

You do not need to wait until you burn out before you take a PURRR. I will talk about that in my next missive.

The more self-aware you become, the more competent you become. Sometimes, I tell my team members, 'If I continue with this project, I'm going to burn out and I don't want us to get to that point as it will affect you and the project. Let's take time off and come back to this after a week.' Some other times, we don't even review until after three months.

Constant practice is required for someone who aspires to live a life of growth and positive impact. Pay attention to yourself as a person, as a professional, and as a business leader. Pay attention to how you respond, pay attention to what affects you, pay attention to how you deal with things, adjust to who you really want to be, and it will connect you to your next phase in life. To get to the next level, you must pay attention to where you are at the moment and more importantly, you need to PURRR from time to time.

11

Growth Pangs

'Everything negative—pressure, challenges—is all an opportunity for me to rise.'

– Kobe Bryant

Dear One,

You must know by now that the entire process of growth is not a walk in a park. A lot of challenges can be associated with growth and the most peculiar is burnout.

Somewhere along the line, even with clarity, you may experience burnout. I have experienced burnout and almost everybody I know has experienced burnout at some point or the other.

How do you know when you are burnt out? One major thing to watch out for is tiredness. It's the physical sense of being tired to your bones. Once you begin to feel like you're not achieving results or you begin to question your sense of worth, you are getting burnt out. It could also be a situation where you feel you are not getting anything done and you begin to lose sight of the results you are producing.

It could get physical to the point where your shoulders are constantly slumped, you experience backaches, headaches, and/or a general feeling of unwellness. Your immune system gets depressed, and your emotions seem all over the place. You begin to feel unworthy. Your patience grows thin or completely disappears, you find it difficult to be patient with yourself or anyone, and you begin to feel a lot of irritation with everything. You get easily irritated, easily angered, and nothing seems good enough. Nothing seems to make sense anymore. You snap at anything and everything, and everybody becomes an enemy.

These and more are some of the symptoms I have experienced and seen over the years. An interesting part of this is, it happens differently for different people.

The thing about burnout is that once it shows up in one area, it's easy for it to affect all the other areas of one's life. When you begin to experience some or all of these symptoms and they go unchecked, they could lead to anxiety, depression, and at the end of the day, you find that you have no energy to even take care of yourself because you're just completely exhausted—physically, mentally, spiritually, psychologically, and emotionally.

> Once burnout shows up in one area of life, it's easy for it to affect all the other areas of one's life.

I recall a period when I experienced burnout. At that time, I was in business school and also keeping a full-time job as well as a part time job. I was working for fifteen hours a day.

I got to a point when I would be awake but not be able to concentrate on anything. I would read emails and wonder why people were asking me certain questions. I would wonder why they were unable to figure things out themselves. I developed an impatience towards legitimate logical behaviour from other people because I felt they didn't know what it felt like to work for fifteen hours straight. I was stressed and felt they were adding to my troubles.

However, I soon got a handle on it and gradually recovered.

How did I do this?

To recover from burnout, the first thing you must have is a sense of self awareness. I already knew myself and when I started the programme, I knew it was going to demand a lot from me. I knew what my threshold was and I was ready to expand or extend my threshold, but I also knew when I was acting out of character.

When I noticed how easily triggered I was getting by reading a simple email, it was easier for me to say to myself, 'Hey, slow down. Why are you taking out your frustration on someone else?'

There and then, I knew I needed timeout to catch my breath. That cranky person isn't who I am and is definitely not who I want to be. I made myself understand that anything that is making me become that person I did not want to be had to go.

Assuming I was okay with being this person who is constantly irritated and tired, that would have been a different conversation. Because I was not okay with it, it was easy to put a stop to it.

I didn't want any of those symptoms to become a part of my life because I was conscious of the programme I was pursuing, and I knew it was going to place me in a position of higher responsibility. If I allowed myself to get used to being irritated at that level, when I got into positions of higher responsibility, it would get worse. So, I knew it was time to pause.

Avoiding burnout is tricky. But it is possible, especially when you know your threshold and ensure not to cross it. However, it depends on the variables.

When I decided to take the programme, there were a number of things that pushed me to make that decision. I knew it would demand me to work more hours, so I gave myself a timeline. I told myself I would do it for only a year and stop afterwards. It is unnatural for anybody to work fifteen hours or more. I know there are people who do it, but that doesn't mean it is right.

Giving myself that time limit was a way to motivate

myself to say, 'This is not who you are, this is temporary. I need to do this and I am just going to do it for this time, but I don't want to get used to it. I don't want my body, my system, my whole being to get used to working and living like this.'

Avoiding burnout means designing your life and your goals such that you are in control of what you do, when you do it and how you do it. When you need to make changes or step up to a higher level, ensure you design that step to be within the timeframe or capacity that you have.

One of the reasons I said it's tricky to avoid burnout is that sometimes, burnout also reveals our capacity for resilience and the things inside us that are untapped.

Thus, rather than avoid burnout, pay attention to yourself and when you get to the brink, stop and PURRR, so that you can deliver without completely sabotaging yourself.

12

Eyes off the Trigger

'To improve is to change, to be perfect is to change often.'

– Winston Churchill

Dear One,

You do know that growth means change, right?

Growth makes it important for you to adapt to change, manage change, and learn from change. This change could be pleasant or unpleasant, planned or unplanned.

One reason we have burnout is our reaction to change. Interestingly, change is something everybody will experience at one time or the other. Burnout can be avoided, but you will get tired at some point.

Identity, purpose and clarity are never static, they keep changing and this is why we must also study the concept of change. The evolving nature of identity, purpose and clarity is what produces change.

So, what are the types of change?

In life, we experience two kinds of change. The first is evolutionary change. This is a kind of change that happens over time; it is a natural change. It takes place subtly and we may not even realise it is happening until we suddenly see the result. It happens gradually, sometimes slowly, but steadily.

The other kind of change is revolutionary. This type of change is abrupt, unexpected, unplanned and sometimes, may be welcome or unwelcome. We are often not ready for it. We just wake up and boom, something hits us that changes our life's trajectory. This kind of change can take one from zero to hundred, or from hundred to zero.

At different points in our lives, we will all experience both, whether in our personal lives, relationships, careers, or businesses. It is not something that can be avoided. It is a part of living.

Since change is guaranteed, it means you can't run from it nor prevent it from happening. Once you have this understanding, your resistance to change will be different. When you resist less, you will maximise more. When evolutionary change is happening, you can see yourself shifting gradually. When that happens, you become a participant in that process. This can only happen when you pay attention to how you want to go through the evolution.

Just like we established when we discussed identity, at some point in our lives, we were children, then we became teenagers, then young adults, etc. These are evolutionary changes, and they affect one's identity.

Not only that, they also affect the names we are called, how we respond to things, how we show up, our priorities, and what we focus on. When we change the things that affect us, the lenses and filters through which we view the world will also evolve.

Once you notice the kind of change that will happen with or without your approval, you have a choice to become an active participant and get more engaged in your evolution. You can become more intentional about the results you want to achieve.

When these changes begin to happen, you can begin to guide your reaction and your decision. Then you begin to master when to clean your filters, when you need to take your lenses to an optician, when you need repairs, when you need to sit down, and when you need to stand up—all because you're engaged in the process of your own evolution.

The Process of Change

Change in itself is about moving from one point to another. It is about movement, whether it is to a higher plain or a lower one. Change involves growth, growth involves change, growth involves movement. They are all interwoven like a loop.

Understanding this would definitely help anyone who is paying attention to change, to grow positively. The fact that change is guaranteed does not mean that the results of the change or the outcome of those changes are going to be positive, because there is also negative change. What will help us determine the outcome that we get from every change process we experience in life is our active participation.

When you are paying attention, are aware, and are conscious of what is happening as well as the results you want to achieve, you will discover how to fashion the situation to give you the results that you want, or at least to give you something remotely close to what you want.

An example is the potter. When a potter starts moulding the clay, if s/he does not know what they want to create, they can create anything and sometimes, it will be good but at other times, it will be bad. But when a potter has a predetermined idea of the object they want to mould, it comes out the way they want it to.

The same holds true as we navigate through life. As we talk about growth, we talk about the change process. As we discuss our identity and purpose, it is like having the clay in our hands, which gives us the power to determine the outcome that we get.

Managing Change

I have seen a lot of people in my line of work who

complain about what is happening in their lives as if they're helpless victims. They do not know what to do. The first question I often ask them is what they want to get out of that situation, that is, the outcome they want.

A lot of times, when people are able to define the outcome they want, it is easier to also decide and work towards the steps that will help them get to that outcome.

If you do not define the outcome you want from any change you experience, and if you're not actively involved in thinking about the outcome you want to experience, you will not maximise the proceeds of growth. I know it is not always easy, but that may be the only option you have. For you to create the kind of life that you want, you have to maximise the opportunities that change brings to you.

I have supported people who lost businesses worth millions in their local currency and that is always a revolutionary change for them. I always ask them, 'How do you want your story to continue? How do you want it to end? Do you want the rest of your story to be about what you had lost? Or do you want your story to be about how you became an active participant in managing the change?' At the end of the day, it is your active engagement in your change that will help you to keep going.

There is an age-long and ongoing debate about whether people change or not. I respect everybody's opinion and I understand people who insist people do not change, but I do not agree with them. I am of the opinion that we all change. None of us is set in stone. We all change in many ways, sometimes in ways we are not aware of. When you are not aware of the areas where you're changing, that's when it's easy for you to negate change.

> We all change in many ways, sometimes in ways we are not aware of.

The fact that you don't acknowledge change does not mean change is not happening. There are many people who go through life without ever acknowledging there are changes constantly happening around them. And because they don't acknowledge it, they are incapable of maximising it. When we refuse to acknowledge change, we are incapable of using it to create the outcome we desire and we end up becoming victims of circumstances.

Even in our relationships, we all change, the person you marry today will not be the same person you will celebrate your first-year anniversary with. By your tenth-year anniversary, the person could be a totally different person from the person you married. However, people often do not pay attention to these things; they expect them to be the same and when they see things that are different, they complain because they have been wired to expect them to be the same.

In some other cases, people expect their partners to change. The thing is, it is easy to demand change from other people, but difficult to do the same work for ourselves.

Adapting to Change

Change is not always positive, especially when left unattended. It could take a life of its own and spiral out of control.

When something unexpected happens to you, it is not the whole story, it is an incident, and it is a trigger. Once that trigger is pulled, a chain reaction ensues, and that reaction is part of the change process.

As you and others react to that process, you might find changes in behaviour, attributes you did not know were there, and many more. When people begin to respond in different ways, they produce different results, different outcomes and these all sprint off from one trigger.

Many times, as humans, we keep our eyes fixed on the trigger and forget that the trigger is just one part of the change process. If you fixate on the trigger, you leave the rest of the change to chance. Thus, your responses may not be connected to a clearly defined objective that will lead to a desirable outcome.

There are people who become distrustful because of something that has happened to them, or they become negatively selfish, abrasive, and rude because of a betrayal or a past experience. On the flip side, there are also others who become kinder, humbler, and gentler because of a past experience. They are able to listen more and extend help to others because of what they have been through.

One's attitude towards the trigger marks the difference between the person who learns positive behaviour from a past experience and the person who imbibes negative reactions and behaviours from a similar experience. The former takes active participation in the process in order to decide the outcome and looks beyond the trigger to get the results they want to achieve.

When I hear people say, 'This is who I am, take it or leave it,' I think they are being disrespectful both to God and to themselves. God made all of us with the capacity to grow, and to be better. Growth is guaranteed for every human. Everyone has an innate ability to grow and to be better. However, only few people consciously activate that ability and hopefully, as you read this, you will look inside you to activate that ability to keep growing and to be better.

Growth, like identity, purpose and clarity, is not static. It doesn't end. It seems static when one is not aware that one can grow and so, one stays stuck, simply flowing with whatever is thrown at one by life and other people.

In summary, the question is not whether change will happen or not, it is about how you handle change and the practical steps required to handle change. The first thing is to acknowledge that change is happening, identify the triggers when they occur, and notice whether they are expected or unexpected, gradual or abrupt. This is only possible when you are self-aware.

When any trigger comes, acknowledge that something different is happening, and take appropriate action to define the outcome you want to get.

13

What's Next?

'Some changes look negative on the surface but you will soon realise that space is being created in your life for something new to emerge.'

– Eckhart Tolle

Dear One,

Not knowing what to do after change has occurred can cause paralysis.

Imagine a child who finds themselves in the middle of a two-lane highway, caught between vehicles speeding towards them with loud horns blaring. What do you suppose that child would do?

As you probably imagined, the child would halt in fright and probably begin to wail, uncertain whether to return the way they came or move forward, except that both lanes would be equally frightening. In most cases, even an adult would have a similar reaction. However, when the initial paralysis wears off, the person would have to move.

Now, imagine that as that child stands transfixed in the middle of the highway, an adult approaches from the direction in which they had come and safely walks across the highway. What do you think that child would do?

When my parents passed, it was a huge tragedy that paralysed me. I was overcome by grief and didn't know how to move forward. Till today, a lot of happenings within that period remain a blur. However, my saving grace was having a model of something I wanted to fashion my life after. I drew strength from the way my mum had lived her life and desired to do more for myself.

From that experience, I learnt that it is important to look for a model whenever you feel paralysed and uncertain on what to do. Looking for models does not mean you have to be exactly like them. What it means is that a model can help you define what you want to do. The idea of models is not for you to copy and paste.

> It is important to look for a model whenever you feel paralysed and uncertain on what to do.

Consider it as a case study where you observe, take notes, look inward, consider what you have, what you've learned, what you've been given, your skills, your personality, etc. You observe again, and take notes, and then you design your own blueprints. Models are very important and that's one of the big roles mentors play.

It is not a question of copying someone, but a case of having someone who can show you beyond what you are currently seeing. Someone who will help you see beyond your paralysis, doubts, triggers and all you are experiencing.

When choosing models, ensure your model aligns with your core values, which means you must also know your core values as a person. Another thing to know is if those core values are in alignment with where you want to get to. Even if you do not know where you want to get to or how far you can go, you must know your core values.

As you identify your core values, you will find out the ones that don't serve you and drop them. Next, find models that will help you create your next templates, your next blueprint, and the roadmap for the journey ahead. It is a journey, after all, and we all need help to navigate the turns.

Navigating change alone is debilitating as it can also give you a false confidence. Get models, a support system, people who can teach you and people you can learn from. When you're paralysed, it is a good time to learn and open your mind.

If you can open your mind, you can open your mouth, and you can open your hand. Opening your mind makes it possible to open every part of your system. One of the ways to open your mind is to constantly expose yourself to teachers.

Teaching is not telling you what to do, it's someone telling you how to find out what you need to do, and how to do it. This is the responsibility of teachers, mentors and models. Your own part of the responsibility is to listen, take notes, and be sure that it serves you. Learn how to do things by yourself, so you can take responsibility for the results you achieve and the outcome you create.

Surround yourself with a good support network—people who can listen to you and people who can help you listen to yourself.

As we navigate change, it's crucial that we learn how to listen to ourselves because until we learn it, we would not be able to identify when we are lying to ourselves and when we're being honest to ourselves. It is important to hear yourself, listen to yourself, and identify when you're making sense and when you're not making sense. The only way to do that is by talking. You've got to talk to yourself, pay attention to what you're saying to yourself, otherwise, it'll just be in your subconscious and you will not know how your thought patterns and self-communication are sabotaging your outcomes.

Your models, mentors, teachers, and support network must be people who love you unconditionally, whether you are getting it right or wrong. They should not just be people who will hail you when they think you're getting it right but cancel you the minute they think you are getting it wrong.

It is important to be honest with ourselves from the beginning. From the point where you are now, start being honest with yourself. Be honest with your strengths, your weaknesses, the opportunities you have and what you can do with it. Be honest with the difficulties and challenges you may have to face and how you can navigate through them. Be honest with the failures, be honest with where you've hurt people, be honest with the things that hurt you. Once you are honest with yourself first, the way you show up in front of all these will drastically change. Not only will you give to others what you have given to yourself, you will also demand the same from others and attract it from others because it comes from your inside out.

I have seen people hide under the guise of authenticity to wreak havoc, hurt people, step on toes, trample on people's rights and humanity because they feel like they're just being themselves. Authenticity and honesty are meant to connect you to the rest of the world.

I deal with a lot of senior management staff in my day-to-day activities, and most of the time when I don't agree with them or when I think they're not seeing things my way, I present my thoughts to them in a different way. One way I start a difficult conversation is by saying, 'Forgive me if I'm wrong but I think...' Another way I may start the conversation is by saying, 'Please correct me if I'm wrong, but I think...'

Through this approach, I'm trying to call you out, but I'm also honestly acknowledging that I may be wrong. Another way to start such a conversation is, 'You may not like what I'm going to say, but I think you need to hear it.' Most times, people will say, 'No, it's okay, tell me. I want to hear it.'

What you give to yourself is what you will attract. A lot of us demand other people to be honest but we're not honest with ourselves; it's not correct. And if we're not honest with ourselves, we cannot be honest with others. And when we're not honest with others, we cannot expect them to be honest with us. Honest people will struggle to be honest with us while we're not being honest with ourselves because even when they're being honest, we are not going to see it. We won't see their honesty and we won't recognise honesty even when it's thrown in front of us because we don't practice it.

When we believe we can't change, we are not being authentic with ourselves. We know it's not true. We know we can change if we want to. We know we can control our emotions when we're angry. We know we can hold back and not say hurtful things. We know that when someone pushes us, we can walk away. Yes, we know. And every time we decide not to do it, we need to take responsibility for our decisions.

Our responses are always our choices. So yes, we can all change. And as we grow and look at the whole conversation around growth, positive impact, living better lives and being better people, it's important that we constantly remind ourselves that change will happen.

For growth to happen, change must happen, and for change to happen, growth must happen; there is always movement during change and growth. And in that movement, we need to find models, teachers, and mentors. We need to be honest and redefine what authenticity means to us. We need to be honest with ourselves first, then with others—only then can we attract and honour honesty. And when you attract honesty, the next thing to do is to honour it.

There are people who trivialise it when they get it. When you honour it, you get honour for yourself. Honour the people who teach you, honour those models even when you don't agree with them, learn how to respectfully disagree. You can disagree honestly, gently and firmly, instead of trashing other people because you don't agree with them, or because they are different, or because they are changing in an opposite direction from you. All of us are navigating growth and movement and change.

Understanding this will also help us navigate how we relate to faith, to family, to friends, and even to strangers. We observe them, learn from them, honour them, gently take what we have been given, and respectfully let them continue on their journey. And those who share journeys, space, life and time with us, we extend to them the same kindness that we extend to ourselves and the same kindness that we want them to extend to us. And that's how progressive and positive growth and change will happen, not only in our lives, but also in the lives of those we lead, those we serve, those who look up to us, those we look up to, and others around us.

14

Beauty for Ashes

'There are many talented people who haven't fulfilled their dreams because they were too cautious and were unwilling to make the leap of faith.'

– James Cameron

Dear One,

What philosophy conditions the way you live?

Mine is mostly from the Bible and it says, *'All things work together for good to them that love God....'* I strongly believe that based on this scripture, everything that happens to me in life—both good and bad—will work together for my good.

I have also seen this play out in the lives of the people I serve, whether in my capacity as a relative, friend, colleague, mentor, an adviser or a management consultant. I have noticed that no matter how bad things get, they can be made to work together for good.

I have seen a company go bankrupt and out of that bankruptcy, a new and stronger company emerged. I have seen entrepreneurs discover better ways of doing business out of terrible experiences. No business owner ever wants to get to that point where they lose everything, but I have seen a hostile takeover happen and years later, this person said, 'It changed my life. If it hadn't happened, I would still be running the rat race.'

I have seen people face life-and-death situations, survive them, and get to the point where they said, 'The accident made me a better person. It was hard, but I learnt some valuable lessons.'

Beyond my faith, I have seen people from other faiths and even some who do not believe in God emerge successful from terrible situations.

Recently, someone I know lost a high paying multinational job and went on to start a business that makes him fulfilled and happy. Now, he has time for his family. We got talking and he said to me, 'Jane, that was a blessing in disguise!' In the first few months after he lost his job, he was depressed and thought his life was over at such a young age, but gradually, he recovered and he can now see everything working for his good.

Therefore, no matter the change I experience in life—evolutionary or revolutionary—it will work together for my good.

This is another reason you must become an active participant in any change that happens to you. If you leave it to chance, stay depressed, get angry, cry, lament, or play the victim, you are never going to be able to do your part in turning that not-so-pleasant situation to something that can potentially work out for your good.

Have the understanding that no matter how bad a situation is, if you consciously believe that good can come out of it and that there are lessons you can learn from it that will help you or somebody else, something good will come out of it. If you see and believe it, you will position your head, heart, hands and legs to do the work and watch the situation turn around. That way, no aspect of your life will stay dormant for long.

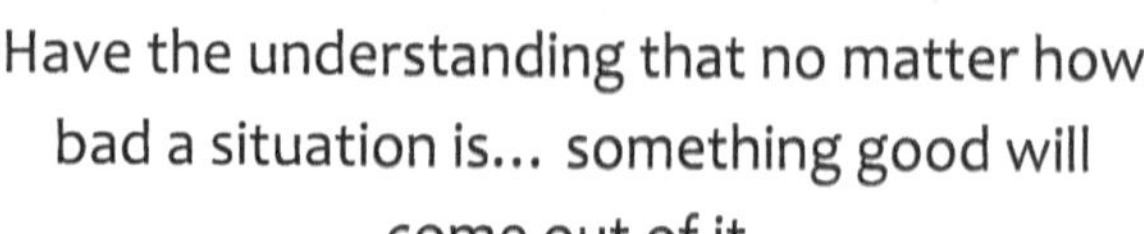

If you look at the seasons, from summer to autumn to winter to spring, each and every one of them have their downsides, but they also have things that are beautiful about them.

In summer, it's awfully hot, yet summer is beautiful because there are holidays, longer days when one can get much more done, time to travel and see friends and do much more, even amidst the heat.

In winter, it is cold and snow falls, yet there's the chance to enjoy cosy dinners with one's family. It is usually not so hot, so one can sleep better at night.

During autumn, the leaves fall and everywhere looks dry. Yet there's the moderate weather and the beautiful colours of falling leaves. That's the beautiful part of autumn and I could say the same for spring.

Just as the different seasons have their best and worst attributes, so will each part of your life have challenging but beautiful things. If you are able to find the place where the not-so-good meets the good, you will find a way to make them work together for your good.

In all these things, there's the chance to learn and find that you are stronger, better and wiser until your time here is done and your full expressions show forth.

Fine-Tune Your Compass

1. What role does self-awareness play in activating the power of pause?

____

____

____

____

____

____

2. How can you employ the power of pause?

____

____

____

____

____

3. Why are you likely to experience burnout?

4. What red flags must you note to avoid burnout?

5. How do you recover from burnout?

____

____

____

____

____

____

6. Recount a period when you responded poorly to change and narrate how you can better adapt to change henceforth.

____

____

____

____

7. How do the changing seasons help you understand the link between faith and change?

____

____

____

____

____

____

8. What philosophy can you embrace to strengthen you in challenging times?

____

____

____

____

____

PART 4

'The path to influence starts with your identity.
Who you are, and who you become, will
determine the impact you make.'

– Josh Steimle

15

Do It, Love It

'The goal is not to change who you are but to become more of who you are at your best.'

– Sally Hogshead

Dear One,

What's your passion? Does it have place in your life?

In my experience interacting with people, I hear some talk a lot about passion. I have heard many people talk about *following one's passion* as if it is the recipe for success. Based on my observation and personal experiences, I think life is beyond passion.

Passion is not something you feel all the time, so instead of passion, I like to focus more on the word 'love.' In all you do, let love propel you. Passion is fleeting; it does not always last. It is temporal, as it comes and goes.

Love gives more autonomy. As you identify and navigate the evolution that growth entails and you do it from a place of love, passion will follow. I am not removing passion from the equation, but I believe that a certain glue is required to keep passion flowing. When you operate from a place of love, it shows your love for your craft, your love for the people you serve, and your love for the people you want to serve you. It's that love that will hold passion together.

Being passionate is fun and games until it gets exhausting. Passion is connected to adrenaline. What people describe as passion is actually a temporal feeling. Passion is great but I think it is absolutely important that we ensure we have the glue that will make passion work in our favour, not tire us out and get us to that place of burnout.

Passion is not purpose! There are people who know their purpose but do not feel any passion about it. They just know this is what they were born to do and they do it. A person who is passionate about something that is not connected to their purpose should not have any business doing it, but because it makes them feel good, they may do it even if it does not connect to productivity.

> Passion is not purpose!

There are others who are connected and have become passionate about their purpose. They feel good about it, they feel eager, and have that joyful readiness to keep working. This is what many of us identify as passion—that joyful enthusiasm and readiness to do something.

The truth is, for it to be sustainable and bear good fruit, it must come from a place of love, otherwise it's going to disappear. You will wake up one day and no longer feel passionate about this, and then what? You find the next passion, the next passion, and the very next passion.

Do you want to be the butterfly flitting from passion

to passion? Do you want to keep doing something you feel passionate about until the passion dissipates and you move on to the next thing? Or do you want to be the person who develops a strong love for something you know you have been called to do?

Even at that, that thing which you have been called to do will also evolve. That idea will keep getting refined as long as you are doing it from a place of joyful enthusiasm.

When people say they lack passion, I interpret it to mean they do not love what they do because if you love something, you will want to do it. I know things I have done for love that I was not passionate about at the beginning. It is mostly when you are doing something out of love that passion comes.

Moving from one passion to another may give you some feeling of satisfaction, exuberance and adrenaline, but how long will it last? How do they connect to where you're going? How do they connect to who you know yourself to be right now? Who do you want to be tomorrow? When you answer these questions, you can then decide how to navigate your passions.

We all have multiple passions. There were things I was passionate about ten years ago that I may not even remember now. About thirty years ago, I wanted to be a medical doctor but right now, I can spend hours talking about business strategy and policy management issues.

Although I love and appreciate medical doctors, I do not fancy being one anymore. Imagine if I had become a medical doctor, I don't know what would have happened, maybe I would have stayed passionate about it. Before I started mentoring, I had no idea what mentoring was, but today, mentoring is one of my passions.

Perhaps twenty years from now, I will become too busy and too tired to continue mentoring. And since our passions evolve as we evolve, it is important to know how the things we are passionate about today connect to the person we want to be tomorrow.

Placing passion above purpose will work against you. It will limit your productivity, focus, and commitments to results. Purpose involves taking responsibility. When you take responsibility for your purpose, whether or not you feel passionate about it, the more you do it and see positive results, the more you will find reasons to enjoy it. For this reason, your sense of responsibility and commitment to a cause must not be entirely dependent on passion.

While it is important for us to feel that joyful enthusiasm, it's also very important for us to remember to honour our responsibility to do what we need to do as long as it connects to the positive big picture.

I do not enjoy ironing but at times when I don't have already ironed clothes, instead of looking for a drycleaner, I iron some by myself. A lot of times, I do not feel like it, especially as I do not particularly enjoy ironing clothes, but I've got to do what I've got to do and it's that simple.

Sometimes, the more you do what you've got to do, you gradually start enjoying doing it.

When I started teaching, it was just because I needed to do it. Passion was non-existent. Thirty years ago, if anybody had told me I'd be in academia, I would have said, 'Impossible!' But I got into education and started teaching and now, I really enjoy teaching. From teaching, I've delved into management consulting, advisory, lecturing in business schools, mentoring, and featuring on platforms that involve sharing knowledge. I enjoy what I do. Whether I'm teaching, mentoring, or consulting, I love my job. There are parts of it I don't like, but I love my job.

Imagine if I had said no to teaching just because I had no passion for it then, I would not be the passionate teacher I am today. When I got into teaching, it was purely teaching and before I knew it, I got into executive coaching. As I found myself coaching more executives, I eventually got tired of it. As I kept digging and learning, I got into management consulting. The more I continued, the more passionate I became. I started getting into advisory roles and it felt really cool as I enjoyed doing it. As I kept digging and coming up with raw materials, I kept polishing and refining my skills, and discovering more things, new product lines, and suddenly, I got an invitation to teach in a business school.

When I started teaching in business school, it was an entirely different experience for me. It wasn't exactly like consulting or advisory because I had to sit down for hours to prepare materials and references for my classes. It wasn't interesting initially, but now I love it.

I do not know with certainty how all of this will evolve in the next ten years, even though I have an idea. However it goes, I will keep digging and opening myself up to all of it.

Give yourself permission not to make passion the entirety of your work, or the definition of what you do or how you do it. You cannot afford to do that because your passion is just one part of it. It's a form of expression of the love that you feel for whatever gifts you have been given or have discovered.

Do you like this gift? Do you think you can actually evolve and unfold this gift and serve the world with your gift? As you start, the passion will come, and you'll get committed to making it work even when you don't like it. Like I explained earlier, I don't like ironing but I like wearing ironed clothes and how they make me feel. That's how it feels like when you are not passionate about something but are committed to doing it well and getting good results.

When you don't feel passion, are you committed to a good result? You may not feel passionate about your job, but does it pay the bills? Do you get the work done? Do you serve well? Take pride in the outcome of your job, be passionate about the outcome of your job and you will do it well. The more you do it well, the more you see how lovely and wonderful your outcome is, and eventually, the more you will forget about passion. With time, you will find other things you'll be passionate about and everybody will be okay.

16

Moment of Truth

'Learning from your past converts into your strength while dwelling in your past makes it your weakness. Making it big is an opportunity but doubting yourself will be a threat.'

– Jayanagarada Shishya

Dear One,

I am glad you have been able to distinguish between passion and purpose. Having determined your passions and your purpose, how can you advance towards excellence?

You are probably familiar with the term, SWOT analysis? If you are not, it means Strengths,

Weaknesses, Opportunities and Threats. This analysis helps in strategizing how to be better as a person in your relationships, job, business, and whatever you're doing in your organisation.

To make headway, you have to know and be honest about your strengths, your weaknesses, your opportunities, and the threats you could potentially face. When analysing your strengths and weaknesses, you look inwards, which is your internal environment. When analysing the opportunities and the threats, you look outwards, which is your external environment.

> To make headway, you have to know and be honest about your strengths, your weaknesses, your opportunities, and the threats you could potentially face.

This analysis will trigger the following questions: Whom do I connect with? Who needs me? Whom do I need? Where can I serve? How can I serve? How can I connect to places to serve? Who can serve me? How can I connect with them? Where can I be of value? What value can I bring? Where can I get value?

When analysing opportunities, seek opportunities for growth, for impact, to serve and to be served.

Having already identified what is going on inside of you through increased self-awareness, you know your areas of strengths and how to maximise them.

While paying attention within, you have probably also identified your areas of weaknesses and you have begun to ask, How can I be better in these areas? What do I need to avoid so I don't get myself or others into trouble? How do I control these urges or habits?

Personal SWOT analysis helps to ensure that you listen to and pay attention to yourself. It leads you to meditation, which helps you dig deeper on any issue you may identify. This process helps you see the need to maximise your own strength, and to know when and how to ask for help.

You may discover the need for a support network, especially in those areas where you can find people who can help. In finding those people, it's important you don't just wash your hands off the process; you must pay attention to what they are doing and learn. Learning in this case may not be for you to learn how to do it like they do but it's also for you to be able to appreciate what they are able to bring into what you're doing.

Again, using the example of my ironing skills, my dad taught me how to iron clothes. He loved ironing and I remember he ironed our clothes weekly. He would ask for our Sunday clothes, school uniforms, outing clothes, and he would iron everything. Whenever he was in this mode, he would sit and have his highlife music playing in the background. You would find him chatting, cracking jokes and laughing as he ironed while we watched him and joined in the laughter.

I still do not like ironing and for this reason, whenever I have people iron for me, I thank them profusely because I appreciate the fact that ironing is not my passion, but they are able to offer me support in that area. The thing is, it is so easy to ignore other people's areas of strength and not acknowledge the effort they put in because it is not your area of strength. However, the ability to show appreciation will ensure that your support network is able to continue to support you. The same way you appreciate them is also the same way they will appreciate your own area of strength, and this appreciation is a very crucial part of growth.

In summary, a personal SWOT analysis will help you identify areas where you are strong or weak, and make you see where the opportunities and threats are. It will also help you identify people who cover your weaknesses and the ones who provide you with opportunities. In doing so, you can better appreciate them and find strength to keep working on your strengths to fight the threats when they show up.

All these are hinged on honesty and authenticity.

17

You Need This Too

'No matter what job you have in life, your success will be determined 5% by your academic credentials, 15% by your professional experiences, and 80% by your communication skills.'

– Unknown

Dear One,

Like it or not, growth will position you before others, whether they come to you or you go to them. Growth will demand that you interact with people. The greater you become, the wider your circle of influence will be, and influence is sustained by communication.

Interaction is communication. It is not just about talking to people, it is also about talking with people. You also need to understand that communication is a two-way thing. It involves listening and talking. You talk, they listen; they talk, you listen.

Understanding this concept will help you because if you don't know how to listen, the way you talk and what you say is going to be lopsided and you will be speaking off your head, not taking people into consideration. For you to serve people, you have got to listen to them. For you to bless people, you have got to sit down with them, listen to them and talk with them.

A few years ago, I started delving into the concept of inquiry and dialogue, asking questions of myself and listening to myself. I have repeatedly highlighted the importance of listening to yourself because that is where it starts—self-communication. For you to be able to communicate effectively with others, you must first be able to communicate effectively with yourself.

As you grow, it's important to understand the importance of self-communication and listening to yourself. These two concepts have been discussed extensively throughout this book. Once you get the self-communication part right, it will be easier for you to replicate it with others.

When you interact with people, start from listening to them and paying attention to what they are saying, feeling, and thinking. As you do so, you'll learn more about people and yourself. That way, you are communicating solutions, help, assistance, blessings, and the gifts that you carry. Sometimes, it is in listening that you discover the gifts you carry. Listening to others helps you identify the solutions you can proffer.

To grow, you must commit to communicating with yourself and with others. However, most of the time, many people focus more on the part of their communication that involves other people such that they neglect or trivialise how they talk to themselves. I implore you to be more intentional about how you talk to yourself. When you do, you will more effectively communicate with other people in your life and sphere of influence.

Alfred Korzybski, a Polish philosopher, said: 'It is critical to be in control of your internal monologue in order to become truly conscious. Your self-talk—the inner dialogue that runs silently through your mind or those you say out loud—can be logical and it can also be illogical. It can be positive, and it can also be negative.'

It is important to ensure that you understand the filters and lenses through which you analyse and sieve information. This will help you attain inner quietness as you talk or listen to yourself. It will also help you identify your triggers and how to respond to them.

It has been said that we teach others how to treat us. I believe this to be true because when you communicate to yourself that a certain behaviour is unacceptable to you, your subconscious will reject that behaviour whenever it is directed at you. Your subconscious self only accepts with ease what it has been taught to accept.

> Your subconscious self only accepts with ease what it has been taught to accept.

It is through our communication with ourselves that we consolidate our guiding principles. We sieve through everything we see, hear or read to unconsciously select what we allow into our minds. The things, thoughts, beliefs, and words that we give space to in our minds define our guiding principles. In return, these guiding principles inform how we interact with others and allow them to interact with us.

I talk and listen to myself a lot. I have learnt to understand what my perspectives are about things and what informs those perspectives. I have learnt to question my voice and to listen again. I have learnt self-love, self-respect, self-affirmation, self-esteem, self-support, self-celebration, and how they align with the sense and purpose of God for me.

Healthy Communication with Self

When I want to address something serious that has to do with me, I address myself by my name. Research shows that when engaging in self-talk, addressing yourself by your own name rather than 'I' helps you to be more self-aware. It also transmits a more supportive and encouraging tone of voice, thereby limiting the feeling of being judged.

There are other studies which show that speaking to yourself in the third person can create a feeling of mental distance that allows for more respect and objectivity that directly enable more rational self-support to follow. It is this rational self-support that helps us to take necessary actions.

Meditation, introspection and mindfulness are tools I use to keep my level of self-awareness high. This clarity helps me define how I communicate (whether with myself or with others)—what I can say to people and what people can say to me. I am able to enjoy and learn from every present moment without judging my experiences and/or responses harshly. I am able to be open, kind and honest with myself while at the same time ensuring that I know where I have rooms for improvement.

I am assertive. I teach myself self-respect when I play the role of advocate for myself. I have also learnt to be firm with myself when there is a need for me to change a particular behaviour. This assertiveness with myself helps me to feel honoured and respected, whether I am calling myself out on bad behaviour or acknowledging and/or celebrating an achievement.

I write. Sometimes in my journal, on my social media pages, and on my blog. There are times when I just scribble on any piece of paper or word document that is open before me. Writing is for me a highly effective way to gain insight into what I am thinking or feeling at that time. Expressing my thoughts in words is like drawing on a canvas where I can view the thoughts in my head or heart and either correct or affirm, as the need might be.

I have a few people whose voices help to remind me of my roots, and I do not take them for granted. While these voices do not replace the voice of God or my own voice, they tend to help me to put things in better perspective. Communicating with yourself is just as important, if not more important, than engaging with others. The truth is that you can only communicate to the degree you understand your own perspectives.

Put another way, recognising your perspectives will directly affect your thought patterns and understanding these patterns is fundamental to understanding yourself as well as how you articulate the patterns in front of others.

In the end, effective intra-personal (self) communication skills will help you improve your interpersonal, social, leadership and communication skills (verbal or non-verbal).

Communicating with Others

As you grow in life and business, you will find yourself facing individuals, situations and systems in ways that can feel increasingly demanding, uncertain, complex, volatile, and ambiguous. With growth comes many positive responsibilities—insights and opinions to share, lessons to teach, conflicts to resolve and instructions to give to the people in your sphere of influence. You will have the need to ask for or be asked for help or feedback. You will also express or receive disagreement or divergent views.

To be able to share any of these things in ways that can help you and those around you, you must communicate them clearly. As earlier established, communication is a two-way process. If it is one way, then it is not complete. If it is not complete, then it is not communication. This is where interpersonal communication skills come in.

These skills include, but are not limited to, the tools you use to let other people know what you believe, think, need, want and feel. In the same vein, you can use the same tools to let other people know that you understand what they believe, think, need, want and feel.

Whether in your personal and family life, in a social group and situation, or within institutional or organisational settings, everyone across all strata of society and industry needs to understand that the only way to meet objectives, positively influence stakeholders, drive growth and positive impact is by leveraging communication.

No matter where you are in your journey to growth and positive impact, you must pay attention to mastering your communication skills. Finely-tuned interpersonal communication skills will ensure you can foster mutually beneficial collaboration, make better decisions, provide better solutions for the ones you have around you and solve more problems. Once you are able to do the above in ways that the people around you can identify with, your level of influence will skyrocket.

Communication and Influence

I define influence as the ability and capacity to inspire an idea, thought, and/or action in others. Influence implies inviting others to change their beliefs, behaviour, and attitudes. Influence directly moves people into action and produces an effect or result without the use of coercion, force or command.

Living a life of impact and influence means that people are already watching and observing you. In communication, people are watching you and at the same time, talking to you and about you. For them to talk about you, it means you have some sort of influence over their time, thoughts or topics of conversation.

You can communicate without influencing, but you cannot influence without communicating. One of the most effective ways I have found that captures the attention of others and subsequently impacts their behaviour is through influencing their emotions.

What emotions do you trigger in people by your words, silence, actions, inactions, and verbal and non-verbal cues? They all affect people in really deep and different ways. How do people feel around you?

The famous Maya Angelou said, 'People will forget what you said, people will forget what you did, but people will never forget how you make them feel.' If you understand this, you will be more intentional about how you communicate with people.

In management circles, the 5 Cs of Communication have been widely shared and taught. They are:

- Clear
- Concise
- Confident
- Credible
- Compelling

In all your communication engagements, ensure your communication is always clear, concise, confident, credible, and compelling. In time, you will begin to see the rewards.

w by now that the entire process of growth is not a walk in a park. A lot of challenges can be associated with growth and the most peculiar is burnout.

Somewhere along the line, even with clarity, you may experience burnout. I have experienced

Fine-Tune Your Compass

1. What unexplored gifts can you serve your world with?

____

____

____

____

2. In line with your responses above, what are your strengths, weaknesses, opportunities and threats?

____

____

____

____

____

____

3. In what areas do you need to improve your communication in order to amplify your influence?

____

____

____

____

____

____

____

____

____

____

____

Conclusion

Dear One,

You made it to the end. Congratulations!

Throughout this book, we have discussed several concepts revolving around how you can better understand yourself, your unique journey, and the different factors connected to your growth process. The aim, as you may have observed, is not to give you a set of generic rules but to help you unravel and discover who you are, how you operate, the resources you possess, what and whom you need, how to attract them, and how to navigate the different stages of your own journey.

This conversation is a never-ending one. It is a discussion every individual must keep going. As you read and meditate on the things I have shared in this book, you will get more inspiration and insights that apply directly to where you are right now in your journey.

While reading this book, you may have discovered that there are many variables and there is no one-size-fits-all. As at the time of writing this book, there were probably things about your current position or situation that I was not aware of. Notwithstanding, this book was written with you in mind and in full acknowledgment of the fact that there are many things about where you are, what your journey so far has been and where you are going that will add to the next phase of your growth journey.

It is my hope that the principles I have shared in this book—which are based on lessons from my personal journey and my interactions with many people in my capacity as a friend, relative, teacher, mentor, consultant or advisor—will provide you with insights that you can apply to make your journey smoother, give you bolder results and magnify blessings both to yourself and to the people around you. When this happens, I shall have achieved my goal.

Now that you have read through the book and taken the exercises, this is my expectation: that you pay it forward by sharing your gifts and lessons with others. I hope you will apply the principles of this book to your peculiar situation so you can bless yourself and everyone around you.

Cheers to your boundless growth!

You may connect with me on:

in www.linkedin.com/in/jane-oma-okoro

⊕ www.themothereagle.com